THE HEINEMANN ACCOUNTANCY AND ADMINISTRATION SERIES
General Editor: Dr J. Batty DCom(SA), MCom(Dunelm), ACMA, MinstM, MIPM.

Managing Your Company's Finances

Managing Your Company's Finances

Richard L. Hargreaves, BA(Cantab), MSc, PhD, ACIS
and Robert H. Smith, CA

Foreword by Viscount Caldecote,
Chairman of Finance for Industry Limited

HEINEMANN: LONDON
Published in association with ICFC
Industrial and Commercial Finance Corporation Limited

William Heinemann Ltd
10 Upper Grosvenor Street London W1X 9PA

LONDON MELBOURNE TORONTO
JOHANNESBURG AUCKLAND

First published 1981
© R. L. Hargreaves and R. H. Smith 1981

434 90686 7

Filmset by Reproduction Drawings Limited, Sutton, Surrey
Printed by Redwood Burn Limited, Trowbridge

Contents

Foreword by Lord Caldecote   xi
Editor's Foreword   xii
INTRODUCTION   xiii

1 THE NEED FOR FINANCIAL MANAGEMENT   1
    1.1 Introduction   1
    1.2 General scope and importance of financial management   1
    1.3 The importance of control   3
    1.4 Forecasting and planning   5
    1.5 Investment decisions   6
    1.6 External finance   6
    1.7 The terminology of financial management   7
    1.8 Action points   7

2 BASIC ACCOUNTING   8
    2.1 Introduction   8
    2.2 Basic principles   8
    2.3 The main components of a balance sheet   11
    2.4 Useful points to note when reading a balance sheet   15
    2.5 The main components of a profit and loss account   16
    2.6 Useful points to note when reading a profit and loss account   18
    2.7 Inflation accounting   18
    2.8 Useful ratios   21
    2.9 Parties requiring accounts   21
    2.10 The auditor, his role and uses   27
    2.11 Example of accounts for different types of business   28

Contents

3 PROFITABILITY — 31
   3.1 Introduction — 31
   3.2 Profit — 31
   3.3 Productivity — 33
   3.4 Return on capital employed — 34
   3.5 Action points — 39

4 CASH MANAGEMENT — 40
   4.1 Introduction — 40
   4.2 Cash flow — 40
   4.3 Working capital — 43
   4.4 Cash flow forecasting — 46
   4.5 Sources and applications of funds statements — 48
   4.6 Management of a cash surplus — 50
   4.7 Action points — 51

5 CREDIT CONTROL (SALES) — 53
   5.1 Introduction — 53
   5.2 The nature of credit control — 53
   5.3 Operating a credit control system — 55
   5.4 Discounts — 59
   5.5 The importance of control — 60
   5.6 Action points — 63

6 CREDIT CONTROL (PURCHASES) — 65
   6.1 Introduction — 65
   6.2 Selecting suppliers — 65
   6.3 Terms of credit — 66
   6.4 Control of payments to suppliers — 68
   6.5 Discounts — 69
   6.6 Surviving difficult times — 69
   6.7 Action points — 71

7 BUDGETARY CONTROL — 72
   7.1 The importance of budgeting — 72
   7.2 Uncertainty in budgeting — 73
   7.3 Basic budgetary control — 74
   7.4 The approach to the design of simple budgets — 74
   7.5 Action points — 76

8 CAPITAL EXPENDITURE BUDGET — 77
   8.1 Introduction — 77
   8.2 What is meant by capital expenditure — 77
   8.3 Justifying capital spending — 78

8.4	Measuring returns	79
8.5	Methods of investment appraisal	79
8.6	Discounted cash flow	82
8.7	Net present value	83
8.8	Example of discounted cash flow	83
8.9	Example of net present return	84
8.10	Internal rate of return	84
8.11	Calculations	85
8.12	Action points	85
8.13	Forms	86

9 SALES AND PRODUCTION FORECASTS — 89
9.1	Introduction	89
9.2	Sales forecasting	89
9.3	Production forecasting	92
9.4	Action points	95
9.5	Forms	95

10 COST BUDGETS — 96
10.1	Introduction	96
10.2	Profit and loss	96
10.3	Monitoring cost budgets	96
10.4	Break-even chart	98
10.5	Responsibility, accountability and flexibility	99
10.6	Direct costs	99
10.7	Indirect costs	101
10.8	Action points	102
10.9	Forms	102

11 BUDGETED PROFIT AND LOSS — 107
11.1	Introduction	107
11.2	A practical exercise	107
11.3	Mr. O'Duction's objectives	108
11.4	The O'Duction budget	108
11.5	Sales budget	108
11.6	Production budget	109
11.7	Capital budget	109
11.8	Materials budget	109
11.9	Labour budget	110
11.10	Indirect costs	110
11.11	Draft financial budget	110
11.12	Budget revision	111
11.13	Action points	112

Contents

12	PRICING		114
	12.1	Introduction	114
	12.2	Profit-based objectives	114
	12.3	Sales-based objectives	115
	12.4	Variable pricing	115
	12.5	Discounts	115
	12.6	Setting the price	116
	12.7	Factors to consider	118
	12.8	Summary	124
13	JUSTIFYING THE RAISING OF FINANCE		126
	13.1	Introduction	126
	13.2	Basic considerations	126
	13.3	New project forecasts and internal considerations	127
	13.4	Time scale	131
	13.5	Security	131
	13.6	Presentation of your case	134
	13.7	What the lender is looking for	134
	13.8	Raising money in times of crisis	136
	13.9	Common weaknesses of propositions	137
	13.10	Summary	137
	13.11	Action points	138
14	TYPES OF FINANCE		139
	14.1	Introduction	139
	14.2	Capital structure	139
	14.3	Availability of finance	140
	14.4	The types of finance and their uses	140
	14.5	Short and medium-term finance	140
	14.6	Long-term and permanent capital	145
	14.7	Stock Market listings	147
	14.8	Government support	148
	14.9	The pros and cons of different types of finance	149
	14.10	Summary	149
15	PROVIDERS OF FINANCE		150
	15.1	Introduction	150
	15.2	Sources of finance	150
	15.3	Choosing your source	153
	15.4	What does the institution expect?	154
	15.5	Summary	155
	15.6	Action points	155

APPENDIX I GLOSSARY OF THE KEY TERMS USED IN THE TEXT	165
APPENDIX II INDUSTRIAL AND COMMERCIAL FINANCE CORPORATION LIMITED	173
AII.1 Introduction	173
AII.2 The scale of ICFC's financing	173
AII.3 ICFC investment: Uses	174
AII.4 ICFC investment: Forms of finance	175
AII.5 Features of ICFC investments	175
AII.6 Other services	176
AII.7 Examples of ICFC finance	177
Index	187

Acknowledgements

We could not have completed this book without assistance from many people whose help and advice has been invaluable. We would, however, like to record our appreciation of the specific help given by the following:

John Fairlie, a consultant and small businessman, Douglas Laing, who runs his own business and Chris Tanner, financial director of a small company who read and criticized the text in draft form.

Our colleagues and employers at ICFC for support and encouragement.

Davina Chambers, Gillian Taylor and Derry Vaughan for typing the manuscript and its many drafts.

Foreword

In recent years the importance of the small business to the UK economy in exploiting ideas and creating jobs has become increasingly recognized by Government.

The manager of a small business has to have at least a working knowledge of, and some expertise in, marketing, production, finance and man management. The job is very demanding and calls for considerable resilience on the part of the manager, and understanding from his family and friends.

One of the most frequent causes of business failure is the lack of adequate financial controls. But financial management is often the function for which the small businessman is least well equipped. Any advice on the understanding of accounts, forecasting, and budgeting, and particularly a cash flow estimation, must therefore be welcomed, and be of real value.

ICFC (part of the Finance for Industry group) which has a unique experience in the risk financing of small businesses is pleased to be associated with the publication of this book at a time when a record number of small businesses are being set up in the UK.

I hope all those involved in managing small businesses, particularly those in the early stages of development, will find this book useful.

Viscount Caldecote

Editor's Foreword

The Heinemann Accountancy and Adminstration Series is intended to fill a gap in the literature that caters for accountants, company secretaries, and similar professional people who are engaged in giving a vital information service to management. As far as possible, due recognition is given to the fact that there are two distinct bodies of readers: those who aspire to professional status—the students—and others who are already managing and or serving management.

The provision of finance to the small and medium-sized company may be likened to the supply of oil and petrol to the family car. Without the essential inputs a vehicle (or company) lurches to a halt and, if overheated, may be difficult to restart.

In providing this introduction to the management of finance, the authors show the need for effective methods of planning and controlling, thus utilizing company resources to the best advantage. This is a book to start directors and managers *thinking finance*; to make them see that budgeting is an integral part of management, that profitability is vital for continued success, and that accountants are available to provide vital information on results and deviations from plans made.

This book is recommended to all who are seeking finance or, having obtained it, wish to ensure that efficient utilization is achieved.

J. Batty

Introduction
Managing Your Company's Finances

For some years we have felt the need for managers of small businesses to have some book to which they can refer for guidance on controlling the finances of their company, planning and raising external capital. Many excellent text books, on subjects such as costing, provide a detailed treatment of specific areas. The aim of this book is to cover in a readable form a wide range of areas of financial management and it is hoped that readers who wish to delve more deeply into areas of particular interest will go to the books listed in the bibliography.

The book is intended to be practical and draws on our experience of a variety of small and medium-sized businesses. In particular we have tried to meet the needs of those businesses whose managers find that they have no-one to whom they can turn for advice. In our work for ICFC we have been impressed with the dedication of these managers and it is to assist them that we have co-operated in writing this book.

The book falls into three natural sections – basic accounting and cash management; budgeting, forecasting and pricing; and the raising of external finance.

The accounting section explains basic accounting terms and concepts and gives hints on how to interpret balance sheets. Simple examples of the accounts of different types of businesses are included to demonstrate the substantial differences between, for example, manufacturing and retailing concerns. We are strong believers in good cash management. The availability of cash to meet demands at a particular time is of vital importance. The profits shown in a set of accounts do not pay bills – only cash will do that. Cash forecasting is a most important yet underused management tool and it is of special value to the small business which has no reserves on which to draw.

The budgeting section is designed as a practical guide to planning in the smaller business. Planning involves estimating capital spending,

Introduction

cash requirements, sales and production levels, profits and pricing. The value of cash flow forecasting is again emphasized.

The widely held view that money is available in the finance system for worthwhile projects has been confirmed by the Bolton Committee and the Wilson Committee in recent years. If there is a gap, it is one of information about the existence of the many varied sources of finance, combined with the inability of businesses to present a convincing case to financiers. The final section of the book deals with the sources of finance and gives some hints on how best to persuade sources of finance to support a project.

Some of the subjects are covered in less depth than we would have hoped because of shortage of space and readers who are experts in their own field may feel that the treatment of some topics is too superficial. We are aware of these shortcomings but hope that they are compensated for by the range of subjects covered and the practical straightforward approach that we have tried to adopt.

It is important for the regeneration of the economy that small firms are set up and can grow, creating wealth and employment in the UK. We believe that entrepreneurs and ideas exist in great numbers, that finance is available to exploit the market opportunities and that small firms are ideally placed because of their flexibility and speed of response.

Encouragement and advice is, however, needed and should be provided increasingly by Government, the City and everyone else who can contribute, as we all have an interest in the health of this vital sector of the economy.

I
The Need for Financial Management

1.1 Introduction

The theme of this book is finance and its management. This involves a wide range of issues, many of which are dealt with in the following chapters. By way of introduction to the more detailed discussions, this first chapter is concerned with a general discussion of the concept of financial management and its relevance to both the day-to-day running and long-term planning of a business. Figure 1.1 illustrates the financial management process which will be discussed below.

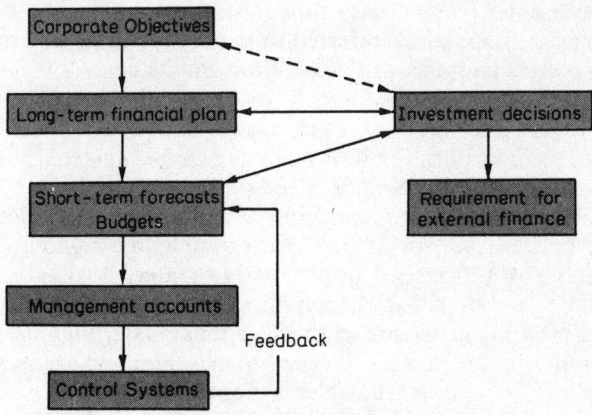

Figure 1.1 The Financial Management Process

1.2 General Scope and Importance of Financial Management

Money is the common commodity used in all commercial life and almost all transactions can be, and usually are, converted into monetary terms. Thus a manufacturing company pays money for its raw materials, pays its staff for their work, pays rent and other expenses and eventually sells its products for money. These transactions usually do not occur simultaneously and hence the movement of money (cash flow) becomes as important as money itself. Financial management involves the overall planning, control and allocation of this common commodity.

In its broadest sense financial management relates to most aspects of a business. It includes the management of the total financial resources available to the business, the management of the business within those resources and all aspects of the decision to invest or not. Management of the available resources involves considerations of raising external finance to increase these resources and, particularly in listed companies (i.e. quoted on the Stock Exchange), allowing for dividend declarations and other distributions which will reduce cash resources available to the business in the future.

Investment decisions will involve considerations such as the absolute profitability of the proposals and the comparison of the possible returns on capital with the risks involved. However, it is vital to be clear on corporate objectives before major investment decisions can be made. In a large company these corporate financial objectives will usually have been thought out and clearly stated; for example to achieve profit maximization. Unfortunately in a smaller company the objectives are often less clearly thought out.

Because the transactions referred to in the first paragraph above do not take place simultaneously, cash flow and its control is one of the most important of all the aspects of financial management. This importance arises from the fact that a company will fail to survive if it is unable to pay its bills, i.e. if its incoming cash is inadequate to cover its payments. This is a commoner reason for failure than accounting losses. The complexity of managing cash flow becomes clear when some of the flows are considered. For example, a common pattern is that credit is taken from the supplier of raw materials (thus cash is not immediately paid on receipt of supplies), wages are paid to the staff weekly or monthly in arrears (cash is again paid later than the services of the employees are received), rent and certain other overheads may be payable in advance (cash is paid before all the benefit is received) and trade customers will almost certainly wish to take credit before settling invoices (cash will thus be tied up in unpaid invoices until settlement is made). Stock and work in progress must not be forgotten either. Money will be required to hold stock and in any company whose manufacturing process is of considerable length, work in progress can become one of the dominant needs for cash. This is because much of the cost of getting the work to its current state will

The Need for Financial Management

have been paid and, commonly, no payments will be received from the customer until some time after delivery of the completed product.

In any period of time considered, the net sum of these cash inputs and outputs will produce an increase or decrease in cash resources and the trend in the sum will determine whether the company is building up cash balances or requires increasing amounts of external finance. The juggling and prediction of the constituent items to manage that net sum within the company's resources represents much of the skill of financial management.

At first sight the cash management skill might not seem a difficult one to acquire. Unfortunately, however, the changing circumstances of a company's business and its economic environment create complexities which can result in enormous problems. At any particular moment it is likely that turnover is increasing or decreasing and thus the average amount of money owed to, and being received by, the company is also changing. Additionally the terms of trade in the industry, namely, the length of credit which companies will allow their customers, may be changing as may stocking requirements due to possible shortages in the industry. Indeed, almost every parameter in the cash flow equation may also be changing. Added to this there may be price increases in materials, labour and overheads such that the costs of manufacturing or selling the products are changing in ways which would threaten profitability unless selling prices are raised by the right amount at the right time. Thus it becomes essential for a company to develop systems which are capable of prediction of future cash flow needs and profitability as well as being capable of measuring the precise state of affairs at any moment in time. The secret is to develop systems which by measuring the current state of affairs and comparing them with past experience and original expectations enable corrective action to be taken whenever any factor in the whole system alters adversely.

1.3 The Importance of Control

It is crucial to both the day-to-day running of a business and its longer-term viability that its profitability in accounting terms is at least maintained. This not only affects the value of the business but is the means by which cash can be generated internally, either to assist with future expansion or for distribution to shareholders. One important aspect of the protection of the profitability of a business is to ensure that unnecessary cash resources are not devoted to running it at any moment in time. Inefficient management resulting in excessive cash requirements can have two consequences. The first is merely that either interest charges are greater or the opportunities for other profitable uses of cash are lost. The second is far more serious in that the company may cease to have adequate cash resources to meet its needs and may ultimately fail.

To say that it is essential to control all aspects of the company's finances to protect profitability and, maybe, the company's very existence is easy. To achieve control is more difficult.

The first stage in the process of control is that of measurement of the important items including orders, sales, costs, profit and cash. It is then necessary to present this information in a way which can be interpreted by management and used to assist action which leads to control. The normal presentation of information is to compare the current state of, say, sales with the position at the same point in the previous year and with the position that was earlier anticipated for the current year. The comparison with past performance is relatively easy as this is a statement of historic information. The comparison with expectation (budget) is meaningless unless the budget has been prepared in a thorough and complete manner – a difficult task – rather than on the basis of blind guesswork. When the comparisons are made, any discrepancy with expected performance will be revealed. This discrepancy must then be broken down in such a way that the reasons for it can be deduced. Even with an apparently simple item such as sales, adverse performance may be due to a number of factors including poor salesmen, poor product design, too high a selling price, shortage of stock, delivery problems and invoicing problems. A more complex item such as profit, on the other hand, requires a sufficient breakdown in the information system to give a firm indication of the area causing the difficulty, so that further enquiries can be concentrated in the correct direction.

It should go without saying, but unfortunately often does not in many companies, that the quality of the information system is not alone sufficient to ensure good control. The timing of the presentation of the information is also vital. It is better to produce a system which gives information on the most important items within, say, ten days of the month than to have a system which gives a fully detailed breakdown but is several months behind time. By the same token a good information system is useless if it is not considered properly by management and used as a basis for corrective action. The medium for such decisions is often the board meeting and it is salutary to learn how many small companies do not hold regular board or management meetings.

In summary, there is no doubt that many companies do not recognise how essential a good information and control system is for

The Need for Financial Management

efficient profit-maximizing performance. Also, in our experience, the most common weakness of the smaller business is an inadequacy of financial control in general and of information systems in particular.

1.4 Forecasts and Planning

It was noted in paragraph 1.2 that the smaller company is often unclear on its corporate objectives. Long-term plans are also not common. They are possibly less important for the small than for the large company. Nevertheless, they serve the important function of forcing the company's executives to think forward and, in particular, to concentrate on the directions in which the business could and should be going. It is fair to claim that any business which does no long-term planning is lacking in control over its own direction which will, therefore, depend entirely on short term views and external changes. On the other hand any plan which does not have general executive support will be ineffective.

A long-term plan might include five year forecasts of profit and cash but it cannot be expected that these will be accurate over the whole period. There are too many uncertainties for this to be likely and the forecasts will require frequent revision. However, the value of this approach is that forecasts are revised against a view of where it is hoped the company will be going rather than on a completely *ad hoc* basis.

Whether or not long-term planning is carried out, shorter-term planning and forecasting are vital functions. The planning process will involve consideration of the means by which the objectives (e.g. target profit, turnover or market penetration) for the period are to be achieved. Availability of plant, cash or resources may be limiting factors leading to necessary modifications before the final or master plan can be finalized.

The process of forecasting is closely linked to planning. It involves the best attempts to estimate probable sales, costs and other factors for the forecast period. Once analysed this information will lead to the preparation of detailed forecasts, the most important of which are profit and loss and cash flows. This detailed financial plan (known as a budget) is the main standard against which performance will be judged. It will require breaking down into control periods (probably one month) to enable control to be achieved by comparing actual with forecast performance. The importance of this ability to control was stressed in the previous section.

1.5 Investment Decisions

Many text books have dealt with this subject in depth and it is not the intention in this book to repeat what others have said. The subject is very large and is often completely ignored by the smaller company. However, there are some points which are worth making.

The smaller company usually does not invest in the continuing manner which is seen in the larger listed company. Its major financial decisions may be few and far between and the alternatives may simply be whether to invest in a particular project or not, rather than to differentiate between a number of different projects. The range of alternatives is often small because of the restricted range of the company's activities and the management constraints which limit, for example, possible diversifications.

Even if a company's major financial decision is simply between whether to invest or not, it needs to be taken with as much care as a more complex investment decision involving many options. Thus it is necessary to be fully aware of how well the company is doing and how well it can afford the risks of new investment. Careful forecasts of the investment project need to be considered to determine, at the very least, whether the project makes the kind of return on capital which the company seeks as a general objective. For most small companies this tends only to mean the project appears 'attractive' and is at least sufficiently profitable to cover the cost of any external capital required. Even if the financial criteria are satisfied there may be strategic, social or even moral considerations which will influence or occasionally dominate the decision.

Needless to say, if the decision is a major one, it must be considered fully and formally at a board meeting. Apart from the value of criticism from all interested parties, it is vital that complete management commitment is made if the project is to be successful.

Lastly, it should not be forgotten that every replacement of a piece of machinery on the shop floor is an investment decision and that there may be alternatives to the simple replacement of a worn out machine by a new and similar machine. Such decisions should also be taken with care as many mistakes have been made by treating these minor decisions casually.

1.6 External Finance

A requirement for external finance may arise from three general categories of need:

The Need for Financial Management

1. existing cash resources being inadequate to finance the company's continued trading or expansion;
2. a wish to invest in a new project;
3. a wish for some or all shareholders to realize a part of their equity in the business.

In some ways this is the most difficult area of all because it involves interaction with a source of finance which means that decisions can no longer be taken in isolation. As soon as a company requires anything other than straightforward short term finance such as a bank overdraft, it will find that the potential source of finance wishes to look closely at the business and the way it is run. Most providers of finance will pay particular attention in their investigation to the general financial management of the business because of the vital importance of this discipline in ensuring the survival and steady progress of a company.

In this book the importance of first making the internal decisions carefully before approaching a possible external source of finance is stressed. Not only will the provider be more impressed with a company which can demonstrate the care it has taken in its planning and decision-making process but this process will inevitably mean that the necessary detailed background information which the provider of finance will require is already available.

1.7 The Terminology of Financial Management

A glossary of the main financial terms used throughout the book is given in Appendix I.

1.8 Action Points

1. Decide on corporate objectives before considering major investment decisions.
2. Recognize the importance of cash flow control; a company will fail to survive if it cannot pay its bills.
3. Develop information systems which highlight problems and direct corrective action.
4. Recognize the importance of protecting profitability.
5. Prepare and present management information properly.
6. Produce management information quickly rather than in great detail.
7. Hold regular management meetings.
8. Make investment decisions with care.

II
Basic Accounting

2.1 Introduction

This chapter attempts to give some insight into the basic principles of accounting and the approaches most frequently adopted by accountants. Some of the material is theoretical and, as a result, is not essential reading for those whose concern is only with the practical problems of the financial management of their company. The chapter does, however, give a guide to the understanding of some of the material used elsewhere in the book. It also aims to provide a practical approach to the interpretation of the information contained in accounts.

The chapter is not intended as an aid with the preparation of accounts. Readers requiring either a fuller treatment of the subject or help with the preparation of accounts should refer to one of the many excellent books wholly devoted to the subject.

2.2 Basic Principles

Accounting is the accepted language by which certain features of all businesses can be described. The features are those which can be expressed in quantitative financial terms. They include turnover, profit, salaries and cash flow. They do not directly include employee relations, quality of product and other aspects of a business which cannot be given a direct monetary equivalent. It is also important to recognize that the language can be employed for different purposes. For example, the two main uses of accounting are essentially different. These are (1) *Audited Accounts;* the periodic presentation of the financial performance of the business by an independent assessor (the auditor) for the benefit of the owners and others not involved in managing the business; and (2) *Management Accounts;*

Basic Accounting

the presentation of financial information about the day-to-day performance of the business in a manner which informs management and which can help them control that performance.

The basic principles which are important to a proper understanding of accounting statements are as follows:

2.2.1 Monetary Measure

Accounting can only record facts which can be expressed in monetary terms. The concept implies a uniformity of monetary values which may not be so, particularly at times of rapid change in exchange rates (if the business uses different currencies in its trading) and inflation.

2.2.2 Entity

Accounting is concerned with events as they affect a specific area of attention. Thus when facts about a business are recorded, the only relevant question is how certain changes may affect the business. How they may affect the persons who manage or are employed by the business is not relevant.

2.2.3 Going Concern

Unless there is good reason to believe otherwise, accounting assumes that a business will continue to operate for an indefinitely long period in the future. This implies, for example, that the fixed resources used in the business will continue to be used for this purpose rather than sold tomorrow under the auctioneer's hammer.

2.2.4 Double Entry

The double entry bookkeeping method, which originated in Italy in the thirteenth century, is universally accepted as the basis for all modern accounting systems. The principle is simple, namely that every event recorded in the accounts affects at least two items in those accounts. Thus if £100 cash is subscribed to a business by the owner, his claim on the business i.e. his equity or capital (which is a liability of the business) is £100 as is the cash in the business bank account (which is an asset of the business). The equality of asset and liability in this example can be generalized in the statement that all assets of a business have claims made upon them by either the creditors of the business or owners of that business and that, as the total of claims and assets must be equal, any change in the one must lead to a corrresponding change in the other. This gives an easy first check on the accuracy of accounting records by totalling all assets and comparing with the total of all liabilities.

2.2.5 Cost

An asset is normally entered into the accounting records at the price paid to acquire it, i.e. its cost. The real worth of the asset may change for a variety of reasons but the accounting measurement has not normally varied, the assumption made being that cost and value do not differ over time. This approach is simple to apply and has had widespread application. However, with the advent of high levels of inflation it has been increasingly criticised as giving misleading information about profit and cash availability in a business. As a result, the accounting profession has moved towards inflation accounting (one version of which is current – rather than historic – cost accounting).

2.2.6 Realization

Most accounts are prepared on the basis that income or revenue is not earned until the goods or services concerned are sold to the customer, i.e. realized. Thus stock in the warehouse is not entered in the accounts at selling price (which contains the element of profit to be earned on its sale) but at cost or net realizable value whichever is lower.

2.2.7 Consistency

It is recognized by accountants that despite much standardization there may be a variety of alternative procedures to handle a transaction all of which may comply with generally accepted principles (e.g. the various methods of depreciation). Thus all such transactions should be dealt with in a consistent manner from the preparation of one set of accounts to another or attention needs to be specifically drawn to any change.

2.2.8 Materiality

Like all quantitative measurement techniques, accounting only concerns itself with events which have a significant bearing on the final outcome. For example a purchase of pencils for the office will be treated as consumed immediately and not as an asset to be depreciated over a period as the figures involved would not affect the profit in any significant way.

2.2.9 Conservatism

The general accounting approach to measurements is to adopt the answer which gives the worst immediate results. This approach leads

Basic Accounting

to rules such as writing off all doubtful items and anticipating no profits until realized. The approach may not always give the most accurate picture but erring in the direction of conservatism has less severe economic consequences than its reverse, as many an ex-owner of a bankrupt business can testify.

The main accounting statements of a business that are prepared both for external scrutiny and internal control purposes are a balance sheet, and a trading and profit and loss account. The main features of these will be dealt with in turn.

2.3 The Main Components of a Balance Sheet

The balance sheet given in Table 2.1 is an example which will be used to illustrate some of the basic accounting concepts summarized in Section 2.2. The balance sheet is presented in a form suitable for discussion; it does not use the more detailed layout as would published accounts.

The principle behind a balance sheet arises from the double entry concept (mentioned in paragraph 2.2.4) that all assets of the business have claims made upon them by either the creditors or the owners of the business and that the total of such claims must be equal to the assets. It is most important to note that a balance sheet is struck at a particular date and gives a snapshot view of the assets and liabilities at that time and that time alone.

2.3.1 *Fixed Assets*

Fixed assets are permanent assets held for more than one year for the purpose of earning profit. They include freehold and leasehold land and buildings, plant and machinery, fixtures and fittings, and motor vehicles which are the essential resources of the business. Some assets (e.g. land and buildings) may appear at valuation if this is significantly higher than historic cost but it is assumed that forced sale of the assets will not be made (going concern concept).

It is normal, however, to show fixed assets at original cost less depreciation. This is based on the recognition that most assets (e.g. a lathe) have a limited life before replacement is required and depreciation is a means of effectively spreading the cost of the asset over its useful life. If it is felt, for example, that the asset may last for five years it is common practice to deduct, say, a fifth of the cost of the asset before striking a profit figure each year, to match the life of the asset to the charge incurred for it in the profit and loss account each year. The amount deducted in calculating profit is known as

Table 2.1 Summary of the main components of a typical Balance Sheet

				£
Fixed Assets	Freehold Land & Buildings			150,000
(after charging	Leasehold Land & Buildings			50,000
depreciation to	Plant & Machinery			200,000
date)	Fixtures & Fittings			10,000
	Motor Vehicles			20,000
				430,000
Less:	Hire Purchase	30,000		
	Mortgage	100,000		
				130,000
				300,000
Investments	Investments in associate companies or unconsolidated subsidiaries			20,000
Current Assets	Stock & work in progress	200,000		
	Debtors & Prepayments	250,000		
	Quoted Investments	10,000		
			460,000	
Less: *Current*	Creditors & Accruals	200,000		
Liabilities	Current Taxation	40,000		
	Proposed Dividends	5,000		
	Bank Overdraft	85,000		
			330,000	
Net Current Assets	(Current assets less current liabilities)			130,000
				450,000
Less:	Medium-Term Loan (Note)	50,000		
	Long-Term Loan (Note)	100,000		150,000
Net Tangible Assets	(Fixed Assets plus investments plus net current assets less borrowings)			300,000
Less:	Deferred Tax			100,000
				£200,000
Representing:				
Shareholders' Funds	Share Capital			
	Preference Shares	20,000		
	Ordinary Shares	100,000		120,000
	Reserves			110,000
				230,000
Less:	Patents, licences, goodwill			30,000
				£200,000

Note: Often the repayments due within 12 months are shown under *Current Liabilities*.

depreciation and the aggregate amount accumulated to date is deducted from the cost of the asset to arrive at its revised balance sheet value. Thus in the example quoted, at the end of five years (when the asset has reached the end of its life) the cost less depreciation will equal zero. The depreciation period (five years here) is usually taken to be somewhat shorter than the actual expected life of the asset (principle of conservatism).

2.3.2 Hire Purchase and Mortgages

Hire purchase usually relates to the purchase of motor vehicles, plant and machinery and fixtures and fittings and is often deducted from fixed assets to give a net figure.

Mortgages relate to a specific property asset and are again often deducted at this stage.

2.3.3 Investments

Investments in private companies are usually shown at cost but subsidiary and associate companies are treated according to detailed rules which are given in any textbook on the preparation of accounts.

Small investments in listed companies are, however, usually, categorized as current assets because of the ease of realization.

2.3.4 Current Assets

These are amounts receivable or items which will be converted into sales (and then cash) within twelve months from the balance sheet date. Current assets include stock, debtors, cash and listed investments.

Of all these assets the one which causes most controversy is stock. The conservative approach is to value it at cost or realizable value if the latter should be less than cost (an exception to the normal cost concept). The going concern concept is vital here as, despite high cost, stocks of partly manufactured goods may fetch almost nothing in a forced sale. Debtors and prepayments (rent, for example, may already have been paid for the coming six months) are often treated together. Debtors are money owed to the business (mostly invoices issued but not yet paid) and provision must be made for bad debts (i.e. invoices which will not be settled for whatever reason).

Investments in companies listed on the Stock Exchange are normally included at cost with a note of market value at the balance sheet date. Market value itself is not usually used because of its volatility.

2.3.5 Current Liabilities

These are amounts owed by the business which are payable within twelve months. They include creditors, current taxation, proposed dividends and bank overdraft.

The major item is usually creditors. These are amounts owed by the business for services and goods supplied to it. They include, for example, raw material supplies.

Current taxation is tax due in the twelve month period. Proposed dividends are not commonly seen in private company accounts but will almost always appear in the accounts of listed companies. The bank overdraft will be the cash book figure, not the actual amount overdrawn. This means it includes such items as cheques written but not yet cleared. It is sometimes forgotten that an overdraft is a current liability. However, even if a business has had a continuing overdraft for years such finance is still at call which means that the bank can demand repayment of the whole balance at any time and without specific notice (though a few hours are normally given to allow reasonable time to make payment).

2.3.6 Other Liabilities

Finally, certain other liabilities which are not due within twelve months need to be deducted. These may include some taxation due more than twelve months hence and medium and long term loans. The figure thus arrived at is conventionally described as net tangible assets, i.e. all tangible assets less all liabilities.

The last item appearing in the top half of the balance sheet is deferred tax which arises from either (1) a difference in the accounting and Inland Revenue treatment of taxation of fixed assets which will not be discussed further here; or (2) stock relief which was a temporary measure whereby certain increases in stock levels could be used as an offset against corporation tax. Treatment of deferred taxation has long been a controversial item with the arguments centring around whether or not, if the business remains a going concern, the amount will ever become payable.

2.3.7 Shareholders' Funds

The principal items here are the amounts subscribed for share capital and the profits retained in the business over the years. In a family business it is also common to see directors' loans treated as shareholders' funds if these amounts are large and are used as base funding of the business.

2.3.8 Intangible Assets

Intangible assets include payments, royalty agreements and goodwill. The latter normally arises as a balancing figure when a company buys another company for more than the net value of assets. The treatment of such assets is a difficult area. They are usually deducted by bankers but they are commonly treated as fixed assets.

2.4 Useful Points to note when reading a Balance Sheet

Much can be deduced about the financial strength of a company from its balance sheet. However, it must be remembered that the conventional balance sheet tends to show assets at historic cost which, with the advent of high inflation, may be considerably different from market value or replacement cost. The assets most likely to be significantly undervalued are property and plant and machinery. Significant undervaluation means that ratios such as gearing and return on capital can be very misleading.

If a company has heavy investment in fixed assets, corresponding long-term loans used to finance their acquisition can be expected or, in the case of plant, large amounts of hire purchase.

Current assets can reveal much about a company's performance. Obvious questions to consider are whether stock is independently verified (despite normal practice, some auditors do not attend stock checks), correctly valued (obsolete stock is of particular concern) and of an appropriate level for the industry (the stock turn ratio given in Table 2.4 is useful here). Debtors should not be too high (see debtor period definition in Table 2.4) and, most importantly, adequate provision for bad or doubtful debts is necessary − but this cannot be deduced from the accounts alone. Another current asset sometimes seen in proprietor-managed company accounts is loans outstanding to directors. As a company is, generally speaking, not allowed by the Companies Acts to lend money to directors further enquiry is always worthwhile.

The major item in current liabilities is creditors. This item needs always to be looked at with care as high creditors (see creditor period definition in Table 2.4) indicate liquidity strain particularly if coupled with high overdraft. However, during the recent period of additional corporation tax allowances via stock relief it has been common for companies to increase stock levels and hence creditors artificially at the year end to obtain maximum relief which distorts apparent stock-turn and creditor-period figures. Also there may be special arrangements with some creditors such as in publishing when a printer gives deferred terms.

Managing Your Company's Finances

Total borrowings (and the mix of short and long term) are worth noting and comparing with net worth (gearing – see Table 2.4). At the other extreme it is not unknown to see companies with high net cash balances. Whilst this indicates great financial strength it also indicates a lack of good investment ideas as most companies can achieve a higher return on capital employed in the business than on cash on deposit.

The lower half of the balance sheet contains two main items, namely share capital and reserves. Share capital can be complex in its make up. Chapter 14 gives details of some of the types of share capital commonly seen, and complexity usually indicates that finance has been raised by share subscription, other than a normal rights issue, for, say, an acquisition. Finally, the changes in reserves are worth observing as it is normal to see a significant proportion (50% or higher) of after-tax profits retained in any one year. The most extreme exceptions to this are some private companies which are profitable but where proprietors draw out all profits (usually as salary) leaving little or no balance sheet net worth; this policy is usually fine until the company wishes to borrow money!

2.5 The Main Components of a Profit and Loss Account

A typical trading and profit and loss account is summarized in Table 2.2. All such accounts start with sales and each account will be prepared to cover a specific trading period (usually one year for audited accounts). As with the balance sheet examples, the layout does not correspond in detail with a published profit and loss account.

The next step is usually to deduct the cost of sales, that is those costs which directly relate to total sales. These include materials and labour used in the manufacture of the goods sold and an adjustment for stock used (or made but not sold). This deduction gives gross profit. This concept is not meaningful in all businesses but, in general, it is the profit on each item sold before deducting general overheads which do not directly vary with the level of sales (they are often called fixed costs). Unfortunately the concept can be misleading, as direct labour is not necessarily paid in this way nor hired or fired to suit varying sales levels.

Another commonly used concept is that of trading profit which is the profit after all overheads except finance charges, and depreciation, excluding non-trading profits or losses (such as profit on the sale of a factory). It is a useful concept in comparing the trading performance for different periods or different businesses.

Finally, finance charges and depreciation must be deducted. This gives net profit before tax. Once this profit has been struck, taxation

Table 2.2 Trading and Profit and Loss Account for a Manufacturing Company

			£
Sales			1,020,000
Cost of Sales			
Purchases		350,000	
Direct Wages		290,000	
Stock and work in progress:			
opening	100,000		
Less: closing	200,000	(100,000)	
			540,000
Gross Profit (47% of sales)			480,000
Overheads			
Repairs and renewals	7,500		
Staff advertisements	5,000		
Travelling	10,000		
Sales costs	25,000		
Transport	17,000	64,000	
Staff Costs			
Directors' remuneration	20,000		
Indirect labour	110,000		
Administrative salaries	17,000		
Lost time, holidays, etc.	65,000		
Employees' national insurance	57,000	269,000	
Services			
Rent and Rates	25,000		
Insurance	8,000		
Postage	4,000		
Telephone	6,500		
Sundry	5,000		
Legal	2,500		
Audit	2,500	53,500	
Finance Charges			
Bank overdraft interest	11,000		
Loan interest	250		
Hire Purchase interest	500	11,750	
Depreciation			
Leasehold property	1,500		
Plant and machinery	2,500		
Motor vehicles	5,000		
Furniture and fixtures	1,000	10,000	
Total Overheads			408,750
Net Profit Before Taxation (7% of sales)			£71,250
Taxation			
Corporation Tax		12,500	
Deferred Tax		15,000	27,500
Net Profit After Taxation			43,750
Dividends			5,000
Profit Retained			£38,750

Managing Your Company's Finances

charges can be calculated, given that, as mentioned in paragraph 3.2, taxable profit does not equal net profit although it is calculated using net profit as a starting point. Finally, the profit after taxation is available for distribution. In a limited company a dividend can then be declared provided the profit remaining is sufficient to conduct the future business of the company. This is retained profit and appears as an increase in the reserves figure in the balance sheet.

2.6 Useful Points to note when reading a Profit and Loss Account

The main indicators of company performance deducible from the profit and loss account are gross and net margin (see Table 2.4) both of which deserve comparison with other companies in the industry and with prior years.

It is always interesting to see the way profit is appropriated (i.e. divided up and allocated to various purposes). Tax is often the most important appropriation and the accounting practice concerning deferred tax is worth studying. After-tax profit will then either be distributed, by way of dividend, or retained. A good listed company may retain, say, two-thirds of its profits and distribute one-third as dividends to shareholders but many private companies retain much higher percentages. Also it should be noted that in proprietor-managed companies dividends are often unattractive to director shareholders compared with salary because of the investment income tax surcharge. This results in many small companies paying directors more in good years (effectively a dividend) and declaring no dividends, leading to a distortion of net margins which are measured as profit after all salaries.

When studying a company's performance a particularly valuable document is a cash flow statement. Published accounts do not give this information in detail, although they do contain sources and application of funds statements which are a very broad summary of past but not forecast cash flow. A cash flow gives useful information on the trend of the company's cash position and its ability to manage its affairs within existing financial resources. Hence the banker's keen interest in it.

2.7 Inflation Accounting

Some of the shortcomings of historic cost accounting have already been mentioned. In times of 10%-plus annual rates of inflation, the historic approach becomes increasingly open to criticism. For example, depreciation no longer provides even approximately for the replacement of plant, which is increasing in price year by year.

Most companies are well aware of the major problem caused by inflation, namely the increased amounts of cash required to finance the cost of assets. Unfortunately, the rate of inflation can be such that this increased cash requirement to, for example, replace stock at higher prices can be greater than the company's ability to make and retain cash from profits. This leads to higher borrowings unless a means of reducing the cash requirement can be found. This particular problem was, of course, the reason for the government introducing stock relief in 1975 which allowed increases in stock levels to be offset against the tax bill which would otherwise have been payable.

As one example of this problem it is interesting to consider a firm of accountants. Such a business typically has few fixed assets. Its major asset is debtors and work in progress. Because the majority of the cost of accountancy work is staff salaries there are few creditors to set against debtors. Thus when wages exploded during the high inflation of 1974 – 8, debtors, which mostly reflect staff costs, rose at or close to the rate of inflation leading to a corresponding increase in cash requirements which, when this figure was increasing at, say, 20% per annum, was not available from profit. This meant that accountants in general increased the speed of billing, began to ask for interim payments and still tended to need to borrow to cover the rapid increases in working capital requirements. Most companies will have observed these changes in the way they were invoiced by their auditors whose financing problems became as acute as any during this period.

The accountancy profession has spent several years discussing the merits of different approaches to inflation accounting. The approach which has finally been adopted is current cost accounting which aims to deal with the effect of specific price changes on individual businesses as opposed to the effect of changes in the general purchasing power of money and it is, therefore, not a generalized inflation accounting system.

The basic approach of current cost accounting is to charge against income the value to the business of the assets consumed during the accounting period. The concept is simple. Its implementation is, however, more complicated. Since 1st January 1980 all listed companies and non-listed companies meeting certain size criteria have been required to show a current cost balance sheet and profit and loss account in addition to the traditional historic cost figures and, in the course of time, it may be that all accounts will be prepared on current cost accounting principles.

2.7.1 Current Cost Balance Sheet

This involves changing certain asset figures to reflect the effect of price changes which will alter the value to the business of such assets. In simplified terms the main such changes are as follows:

1. property at market value;
2. other fixed assets at current replacement cost less depreciation;
3. stock at the lower of current replacement cost and market value.

The other side of the balance sheet then needs a new reserve called a current cost reserve to reflect the revaluation surpluses and other adjustments.

2.7.2 Current Cost Profit

Current cost operating profit is obtained from the historic cost trading profit before interest by making three adjustments. These are:

1. A depreciation adjustment. This allows for the effect of price changes when determining what proportion of the fixed assets have been consumed in the business.
2. A cost of sales adjustment. This allows for price changes when calculating the charge against income of stock used in the accounting period.
3. A monetary working capital adjustment. Working capital does not just include stock but also involves debtors which are offset to a degree by creditors. The adjustment therefore reflects the effect of price changes on the debtors-minus-creditors difference.

Without going into detail, these three adjustments are the method which has been adopted for calculation of current cost profit. They involve the recognition of changes in value of fixed and current assets and have in mind the maintenance of the necessary capital to run the business at the same level of output before regarding any surplus as profit which can be distributed. Maintenance of capital is a concept that does not appear in historic cost accounting.

To obtain the *current cost profit attributable to shareholders* interest is deducted and a final 'gearing' adjustment is made. Where there are borrowings in the balance sheet which are fixed in monetary terms the repayments are not affected by changes in asset value. This gives the shareholders a benefit which is not shown in the current cost operating profit and a 'gearing' adjustment must be made to reflect this.

Basic Accounting

2.7.3 Simple Example of Historic Cost versus Current Cost Accounts

Table 2.3 illustrates some of the significant differences which can result from adopting an historic or a current cost approach to accounting. It is not intended that the current cost example can be fully derived from the historic cost example as not all the required information is available. Rather, the comparison is given as an example of the differences which can occur. As with the historic example, the precise layout of this example is not the same as would appear in published accounts.

The balance sheet differences reflect the differences in the basis of valuation of assets under the two conventions. These can be large. The difference in the two profit figures can be enormous; in the example the historic cost figure of pre-tax profit is £71,250 which reduces to £32,750 in the current cost calculation. It is interesting to see that in this case the tax charge now almost equals the current cost profit before tax.

2.8 Useful Ratios

Ratios are commonly used for judging the performance of a business. They facilitate a ready comparison of particular aspects of the performance both of a business at different times and also between different businesses at the same time. Many ratios are in common use but they can only be used as a guide to aid management judgement; final decisions will rely on further information. Too much reliance on the absolute figures resulting from ratio analysis can be misleading and generalizations can easily, and dangerously, be adopted. The greatest value of ratios comes from the ease of comparison with other businesses or observing a trend in the performance of a business over time.

A number of the most common and useful ratios are listed in Table 2.4 with brief explanatory notes. It must be emphasized that most of these ratios are capable of definition in more than one way; complete standardization does not exist.

2.9 Parties Requiring Accounts

2.9.1 Shareholders

The Companies Acts require audited accounts to be prepared at regular intervals (annually, in general). Such accounts are particularly

Table 2.3 An Example of Current Cost Accounting

These figures can be compared with those in Tables 2.1 and 2.2 as they are a possible current cost accounting equivalent of that historic accounting example. The numbers which are different are printed in italics for ease of comparison.

Current Cost Balance Sheet

				£
Fixed Assets	Freehold Land & Buildings			*200,000*
	Leasehold Land & Buildings			50,000
	Plant & Machinery			*300,000*
	Fixtures & Fittings			*15,000*
	Motor Vehicles			30,000
				595,000
Less:	Hire Purchase	30,000		
	Mortgage	100,000		
				130,000
				465,000
Investments	Investments in associate companies or unconsolidated subsidiaries			30,000
Current Assets	Stock & work in progress	*220,000*		
	Debtors & Prepayments	250,000		
	Quoted Investments	10,000		
			480,000	
Less: *Current Liabilities*	Creditors & Accruals	200,000		
	Current Taxation	40,000		
	Proposed Dividends	5,000		
	Bank Overdraft	85,000		
			330,000	
Net Current Assets	(Current assets less current liabilities)			*150,000*
				645,000
Less:	Medium-Term Loan	50,000		
	Long-Term Loan	100,000		150,000
Net Tangible Assets	(Fixed Assets plus investments plus net current assets less borrowings)			*495,000*
Less:	Deferred Tax			100,000
				£395,000

Representing:

Shareholders' Funds

	Share Capital			
	Preference Shares	20,000		
	Ordinary Shares	100,000		120,000
	Reserves			
	Capital Maintenance Reserve	233,500		
	Other Reserves	71,500	(note)	305,000
				425,000
Less:	Patents, licences, goodwill			30,000
				£395,000

Note: This difference arises from the different profit and loss accounts.

Current Cost Profit and Loss Account £

Profit before interest and taxation on the historical cost basis (from Table 2.2)			83,000
Less: Current cost operating adjustments:			
1 *Depreciation Adjustment*			
Proportion of fixed assets value consumed in the year	90,000		
Less: Depreciation already charged	70,000		
		20,000	
2 *Cost of Sales Adjustment*			
Value of stock used	120,000		
Less: Historic cost of stock used	100,000		
		20,000	
3 *Monetary Working Capital Adjustment*			
Change in debtors less creditors over the year		8,000	
			48,000
Current Cost Operating Profit			35,000
Interest Payment		11,750	
Less: Gearing Adjustment		9,500	
			2,250
Current Cost Profit Before Taxation			£32,750

Table 2.4 Useful Ratios

1 *Performance Ratios*

Name	Definition	Use
Return on capital employed	Pre-tax profit plus interest paid divided by issued capital, reserves, borrowings and deferred tax Alternatively defined as pre-tax and pre-interest profit divided by the total assets used in the business	This is a broad overall ratio. It gives an indication of the return on investment and is used in comparing alternative investment opportunities. It is a complex ratio which can be defined in a number of differing ways, e.g. return on shareholders' equity rather than total capital employed is sometimes used
Profit Margins: (1) gross (2) net	(1) gross profit divided by turnover (2) net profit before tax (and sometimes interest for investment purposes) divided by turnover	(1) gives an indication of the marginal profitability of the business as well as the degree of competition in the industry (2) gives an indication of the efficiency of the company and, again, typical values vary from industry to industry mostly due to competition or price of entry into the market
Stock turn	Turnover less gross profit (i.e. turnover at stock cost) divided by the balance sheet stock figure	This ratio (where appropriate) gives an indication of stock control efficiency. High stock turn indicates high efficiency and implies lower stock holding costs than low stock turn (less space and finance required)
Average debtor period	Debtors divided by sales for the period. The ratio is usually converted to a number of days rather than expressed as a percentage of the period	The absolute figure is very different from industry to industry. Comparative figures (and trends) give an indication of the efficiency of the company's debt collection
Average creditor period	Creditors divided by sales less gross profit (i.e. sales expressed at cost equivalent). The ratio is usually converted to a number of days rather than expressed as a percentage of the period	The absolute figure is very different from industry to industry. Comparative figures (and trends) give an indication of the efficiency of the company's use of credit and may reveal overstretching due to cash shortage

2 Financial Status Ratios

Gearing or borrowing ratio	Total borrowings including long term loan and bank overdrafts divided by shareholders' funds	The ratio gives an indication of the degree of exposure to (1) changing interest rates; (2) the problems of raising further finance – high gearing implies that all available security is already charged to lenders. Low gearing is seen as a measure of a company's financial strength
Income gearing	Loan and overdraft interest divided by profit before tax and interest. Usually expressed as a percentage	This gives a specific guide to the company's exposure to (1) changing interest rates; (2) the danger of being unable to pay loan interest when profits drop
Current Ratio	Current assets divided by current liabilities. It is often called the 2 to 1 ratio which may be misleading	This gives a general indication of the company's liquidity, i.e. the ease with which current liabilities can be met from the conversion of current assets to cash
Acid test	Current assets less stock divided by current liabilities. It should be at least 1 : 1 in many businesses	This is a more demanding liquidity test than the above as it assumes stock is not readily convertible into cash in comparing current assets with current liabilities

3 Other Ratios

The following are so universally used in describing listed companies and companies to be acquired that they are worth noting

Price earnings ratio (P/E ratio)	The value of a company (i.e. price to be paid or listed price per share multiplied by the number of shares in issue) divided by profits after tax	A useful measure for comparing the valuation basis of one company with another as it gives an indication of return on the purchaser's money. It contrasts with the approach of comparing price to be paid with the net value of assets acquired. In practice a purchaser would consider both factors
Dividend cover	Profits after tax divided by dividends	This gives an indication of the security of the dividends declared, i.e. whether they are at risk if profits fall

necessary for shareholders. This arises from the need to prepare independently verified accounts for the benefit of the owners who are not involved in managing the business. Audited accounts, which usually disclose the minimum information required by law, are often criticised as not always giving all the information shareholders might hope to receive and the trend has recently been towards increasing disclosure. Nowadays it is also increasingly accepted that other parties have a proper interest in the financial affairs of a company and these are mentioned below.

2.9.2 Inland Revenue

The computation of corporation tax and other tax payable by a company cannot be made from audited accounts alone as insufficient detailed information is provided. However, the corporation tax computation does start from the audited profit which is then adjusted as necessary to obtain taxable profit and the Inspector of Taxes has, therefore, a keen interest in the accounts.

2.9.3 Borrowers

A company may have all manner of borrowings, almost inevitably including a bank overdraft. All borrowers will wish to see accounts to check on the company's progress and to check that the borrowings are not at greater risk than was envisaged at the time of their advance. The greatest concern to the borrower is that the company is still making adequate profit to repay his loan. A more particular interest will arise in some complex loan situations where, as a condition of the finance, the company may have covenanted, for example, not to borrow more than a certain amount of money in total or not to sell certain assets. The accounts will then serve as independent verification that these covenants have not been breached.

2.9.4 Managers

For good management, audited accounts usually only serve as a periodic verification of the accuracy of their own internal accounting. To them frequent (often monthly) internal accounts are an important tool to aid control of the business. Indeed management is, as a general rule, the only party in a position to prepare and consider accounts which are more frequent and detailed than audited accounts.

2.9.5 Creditors

Trade creditors often take considerable risks in effectively advancing unsecured and interest free money to the company which is likely to be lost in the event of failure of the business. In return they do, of course, hope to make profit by selling their products on a continuing basis. Major creditors will usually obtain copies of filed accounts from Companies House. However, many progressive companies send copies of newly audited accounts to creditors as a gesture of goodwill.

2.9.5 Employees

Increasingly trade unions are beginning to look closely at audited accounts during wage negotiations. Recently instances have been seen of major firms of accountants being retained to advise a union on the size of wage claim which could be afforded. This trend is to be welcomed, as the most persistent problem in the past has been for employees to demand unreasonably high wages either without seeing accounts or without understanding that profits cannot wholly be devoted to pay rises. Many progressive listed companies now publish in their accounts information, additional to that required by law, which is specifically intended to assist their employees (and sometimes the general public) in understanding the published figures. For example a pie chart showing the allocation of profit between capital investment, dividends, staff bonus payments, etc., is often given.

2.10 The Auditor, his role and uses

The Companies Acts require a company to prepare audited accounts annually. These are accounts which must be independently verified by an auditor who must either sign the accounts as representing a 'true and fair' view of the affairs of the company or state his reason for not being able to do so (such accounts are known as 'qualified').

Nowadays, the auditor is usually not only a qualified accountant but a partner in a firm of such accountants. In the most limited sense his role is to attend the company annually to verify independently all items included in the accounts. This will normally involve his attendance at the stock check, verification of debtors and creditors and a check on all other assets and liabilities. The resulting accounts, once signed by the directors and auditor, must be registered at Companies House and, thereby, become available to all.

However, an auditor can have a much broader role than an annual attendance at the stock take. A good auditor will wish to satisfy himself on the adequacy of the company's financial systems and controls and the sensible company will welcome his advice on this and other financial matters. Advice is increasingly required on taxation, which is a complex matter, and a good firm of accountants will have far more detailed and up-to-date knowledge than any company financial director can hope to achieve.

Managing Your Company's Finances

In the most progressive company/auditor relationships, the auditor becomes involved in all major financial matters as adviser and, through specialists in his firm, a source of expert knowledge on areas which the company cannot hope to know in depth.

2.11 Example of Accounts for Different Types of Business

Table 2.5 gives a simplified comparison between the balance sheets and profit and loss accounts (on an historic basis) for typical small businesses falling into the following categories:

1 Manufacturing
2 Wholesaling
3 Retailing
4 High Technology

These examples illustrate the differences in how profit is made in different businesses, even if net profit is the same (here 2%).

2.11.1 *Manufacturing Business*

The Gross Profit of 35% reflects the considerable added value in a manufacturing business. The business has a product or an idea and will spend a little money in developing it. It needs a sizeable gross profit to cover selling and administration costs. Freehold or long leasehold properties are the rule with manufacturers. The buildings and plant represent the vital assets in the business and are likely to be owned outright.

Stocks of raw materials and work in progress often represent three or four months of work depending on the length of the manufacturing cycle, and debtors are often three months old. The 'debtors' figure shown in the balance sheet is perhaps a little high but it is meant to represent the sales of the last three months in this growing business. If debtors were reduced creditors would be paid off. Stocks in seasonal manufacturers will move up and down sharply relative to annual turnover.

2.11.2 *Wholesale Business*

High turnover, quick stockturn and low gross margins are the key elements of the wholesaling business. Again the property is likely to be freehold. Gross profits are lower than in manufacturing because there is a lower added value. The wholesaler is breaking bulk or holding stock and this service is at less of a premium than manufacturing a particular product.

Because percentages have been used in all cases some useful

Basic Accounting

Table 2.5 Examples of Accounts for Different Types of Business Balance Sheets

	Manufacturing	*Wholesaling*	*Retailing*	*High Technology*
		Percentages		
Fixed Assets	50	40	–	10
Intangible Assets (Patents, knowhow)	–	–	–	30
				40
Current Assets				
Stock and work in progress	50	60	140	60
Debtors	40	40	10	40
Gross Current Assets	90	100	150	100
Less: Creditors	30	30	40	30
	60	70	110	70
Less: Overdrafts and Short Term Loans	10	10	10	10
Net Current Assets	50	60	100	60
Net Tangible Assets (before deducting long term loans)	100	100	100	100
Profit and Loss Account Ratios (expressed as percentages) of various factors to sales				
Sales	100	100	100	100
Gross Profit	35	18	25	50
Accommodation	(Freehold)	(Freehold)	(Rented) 8	Negligible
Selling	7	3 } Wages	8	12
Administration, etc.	10	8 }		6
R & D	1	–	–	10
Depreciation	5	Negligible	–	5
Profit Before Tax	2	2	2	2
Finance	10	5	7	15

comparative information is missing. For example the ratio of stocks to sales is very much lower than in a manufacturing business. A wholesaler cannot afford to have slow moving stocks with the low gross margins available.

2.11.3 Retailing Business

Properties are often on short leases to allow maximum flexibility and mobility. Shop fittings would often be shown under fixed assets. The

Managing Your Company's Finances

significant feature here is low debtors (because of the cash nature of the business and high stocks).

2.11.4 High Technology Business

Very high gross profits reflect the uniqueness of the product and the need to cover very high research and development costs and selling expenses. Often intangible assets (e.g. patents, knowhow) are shown among fixed assets.

III
Profitability

3.1 Introduction

The profitability of a business is, perhaps, more important than any other factor in determining its health and likely future. A commercial operation can only survive if it is profitable, and success is usually measured in terms of the size and growth of profit. Without profit, expansion cannot be financed and a return on their investment cannot be made to shareholders. An understanding of profit, therefore, is of vital importance to any businessman.

The question of how profitable the business should be is a fundamental policy issue. The answer can only be obtained from reasonably clear corporate objectives (see paragraph 1.1) which will need to reflect considerations such as return on capital, return versus risk, and other factors discussed in this chapter.

3.2 Profit

If an individual buys a car for £1,500 and immediately resells it for £2,000 he would consider that he had made £500 profit. Unfortunately, business life is more complex, as there are overheads and other expenses to add to the cost of a product before profit can be calculated. This is not the end of the matter either, as provision must be made for the replacement of those business assets which are required for the company to trade and for possible losses due to bad debts and similar problems. Thus profit calculations for a trading enterprise are far from simple.

Unfortunately, differing views are held on the details of the calculation of profit by members of the legal, the accounting, and the commercial communities and indeed between members within each community. For this reason any profit and loss calculation needs to be examined with care, particularly if comparisons are to be made.

Legally, the original share capital of a company cannot be returned to the shareholders without the express sanction of the courts. The legal profession mostly concerns itself with whether or not this requirement of the Companies Acts has been breached. Most legal cases on the subject have been concerned with whether or not any dividends declared have reduced the original share capital and there is no single agreed definition of profit which can legally be declared as a dividend.

The accountancy profession does not have a simple agreed definition of profit either. Much of the accountant's difficulty in calculating profit is in deciding on the appropriate amount to provide for the wearing out or obsolescence of fixed assets used in the business and the amount to provide for bad or doubtful debts or investments.

The businessman's view may differ yet again. For example, a small businessman may be inclined to take a simple view of profit and to regard any cash surplus at the end of each year as profit. It is also interesting to note two situations which are commonly seen. First, there are many small companies which own freehold or long leasehold property bought many years ago, and never revalued, which is now worth many times original cost. It is not unusual to find that although such a company has made little or no trading profit over its lifetime it would make a considerable profit if it sold its property. A second and increasingly frequent occurrence during the recent years of high inflation is for a company to be making accounting profits and yet, despite no dividends, for its retained profits to be inadequate to finance the impact of inflation on stock, debtors and fixed asset costs. This problem arises from the use of historic cost conventions for calculating profits during times of high inflation. It will no doubt remain in some degree for many years whilst the accounting profession and investment analysts adjust to accounting for inflation.

In summary, profit is a difficult concept. Most of the difference between the schools of thought centres around depreciation and other provisions which can sometimes have a dramatic impact on the profit figure. Inflation has also drawn attention to the importance of asset valuations which change over the accounting period. A good example of the significance of the amount of depreciation is a rental company (e.g. televisions or plant hire) where the number of years over which the rented assets are written off is crucial to the level of profit shown because of the high levels of fixed (rented) assets leading to large depreciation charges, as shown in Table 3.1.

Not only are the profit figures significantly affected by the rate of

Profitability

Table 3.1 Rentals Limited

	Year 1	Year 2	Year 3
Total Rented Equipment cost (no depreciation)	£200,000	£400,000	£600,000
Profit Before Tax and Depreciation (A)	£100,000	£150,000	£200,000
Depreciation (B)			
(i) 3 year write-off	£66,666	£133,333	£200,000
(ii) 4 year write-off	£50,000	£100,000	£150,000
(iii) 5 year write-off	£40,000	£80,000	£120,000
Profit Before Tax: (A−B)			
(i) 3 year write-off	£33,334	£16,667	£ −
(ii) 4 year write-off	£50,000	£50,000	£50,000
(iii) 5 year write-off	£60,000	£70,000	£80,000

depreciation but also the 3 and 5 year write-off periods show, in this example, opposite trends.

Finally, it should not be forgotten that accounting profit and taxable profit (the profit on which tax will be charged) are often very different. The reason is that the tax rules concerning depreciation and other expenses are different from accounting conventions. For example, plant and machinery is 100% depreciated in the year of purchase for tax purposes (i.e. a 100% tax allowance is given) whereas only 20%, say, may be depreciated in the accounts. Thus if a company makes £100,000 profit before charging £20,000 depreciation on a new £100,000 piece of plant with an expected life of five years, its accounting profit is £80,000 and its taxable profit nil.

3.3 Productivity

Productivity can be simply defined as the ratio of output to input. In a company, output is turnover whereas input is the company's resources which are land, buildings, materials, plant, equipment and staff. The ratio becomes higher if more output is achieved from the same input or if the same output is achieved with less input. It is thus a measure of the company's efficiency. Increasing productivity also has a direct impact on profit, hence its relevance to this chapter.

All the factors need to be considered with care and frequently reviewed but the term 'productivity' is nowadays more often used to refer to the output from the company's manpower resources, i.e. how to get more output from the same people or the same output from fewer people.

Managing Your Company's Finances

If an increase in productivity is sought it is common, in a sizeable company, to use work-study techniques to examine the organization of the labour force in a detailed manner. A typical list of areas which might deserve study is as follows:

1. Waiting and wasted time for machine operators.
2. The level of skill of all staff. This may involve training and higher quality recruitment.
3. Better performance. This usually involves better supervision.
4. Performance linked incentives. The attraction of paying employees more if they can produce more in a given time is that the employee benefits from higher income and is motivated to produce more and, if the arithmetic is done correctly, the company's profits increase despite the higher wage bill because of the relatively high profit on marginal output (overheads having already been recovered).
5. Labour turnover. A high turnover rate involves heavy training costs and lower efficiency from inexperienced staff.

For further discussion of this topic reference should be made to one of the books devoted to the subject.

3.4 Return on Capital Employed

3.4.1 Definition

Return on capital employed has already been defined, in Table 2.4, and briefly discussed. The definition given, which is not the only one used, was profit before tax and interest divided by total capital employed (i.e. for a limited company; share capital, reserves, deferred tax and borrowings).

The importance of this ratio can be summarized as follows:

1. The fundamental efficiency in profit terms of companies within an industry can be compared. The Centre for Inter-Firm Comparison publishes comparative company statistics which include this ratio.
2. Provided profits and assets employed can be calculated, the ratio enables the profitability (and efficiency in terms of asset utilization) of different divisions of a company to be assessed.
3. It is a valuable comparative measure in making new project decisions (i.e. to build a new factory or instal a new machine), particularly in considering various alternatives only one of which can be adopted.
4. It enables a ready definition of target profitability to be defined as the basis for forward forecasting.

Profitability

The ratio does, of course, have its drawbacks. These include the following:

1. The definition itself poses conceptual problems of which assets to include. In particular, the assets employed (as per the balance sheet) can be significantly changed by leasing. Thus a leased building will tend to increase the ratio compared to a similar situation with a freehold, as it is likely the reduction in assets will be proportionately less than the profit reduction due to the leasing payments. If plant is also leased the comparative value of the ratio is seriously diminished.
2. There is always a danger in attempting to draw definitive conclusions from the study of a single figure. This ratio should, therefore, not be studied in isolation.
3. It was pointed out in Section 2.8 that too great a reliance on ratios in general can, in itself, be dangerous. Ratios are excellent for initial comparisons as they can highlight areas of interest. Further enquiry will almost always be needed before management decisions can be made.

3.4.2 Return versus Risk

The significance of a comparison of return with risk arises from the fact that an investor will often be prepared to risk some or all of his money if there is a chance of making more money than he could do if he did not accept the risk. At the extreme this is why a person will risk losing all his money time and time again on the football pools in return for the slimmest of chances of winning a fortune. This is an example where the reward may be many hundreds of thousands of times greater than the investment but the risk of failure is roughly as high. At the opposite extreme an investor will accept a comparatively low return if he can be certain the risk of loss is negligible. Thus a guaranteed return of a few percent per anum may be adequate on money deposited in a bank.

The same principles apply to a business situation with the emphasis on whether the expected returns from a project justify the risks associated with the investment. In theory it seems easy to suggest that all that is then required is to calculate potential return and compare with a calculation of risks to arrive at a definitive answer of whether or not to invest. Unfortunately, investment analysis is seldom as simple as this. First, the answer to the computation strictly speaking only leads to an answer which is valid statistically. In other words, many such investments must be made before an average return (rather than a particular loss) can be certain. For example, let us assume the potential return is 210% when the chance of failure is 50%. On average half of all such investments will be lost but half will show a 210% return; of this 100% of the return will go to replace a lost investment and 100% will recover the successful investment leaving an average return of 5% (averaging the remaining 10% over all investments including those lost).

This will only become true when many investments are made. Any one investment may be totally lost *or* show a 210% return.

The first problem, then, when a company is considering one investment or a limited number, centres around whether the company can afford to risk all or some of its money, i.e. some projects may be too risky despite high potential returns. This is likely to be true if, say, a successful business making £100,000 profit per annum buys a business losing £200,000 per annum for a nominal sum. If the acquired business can be turned round to make £200,000 the return on the nominal investment will be enormous. However, if the turnround fails the acquired business' losses may be sufficient to bring down both businesses. Thus, the proprietor of the first business has risked all he has built over many years in an attempt to treble his profits. As a generalization any project which risks the existence of a sound business would be considered unacceptable by reasonably prudent management.

The second problem is the difficulty of calculating both return and risk. Considering return first, some of the possible calculation uncertainties may be as follows:

1. The market and the likely degree of penetration for the product may be hard to measure (especially if the product is new).
2. The company's sales force may not accurately be able to forecast how quickly the product can be sold particularly in the early stages.
3. There may be production (or supply) difficulties involving unforeseen additional cost and delays.
4. Competitors may enter the market at lower prices, thus reducing returns if prices must be lowered.

However, in many ways it is easier to arrive at a sensible estimate of return than it is to quantify risk. It is, however, usually relatively easy to identify potential risk areas which may include the following:

1. The consumer may not buy the new product.
2. Costs may change and render the venture unprofitable.
3. New plant and machinery may not work properly.
4. Market prices may alter dramatically due to some competitors' better and cheaper product (new technology for example).

Profitability

5   The company's management may not be capable of coping with the difficulties of the new project.
6   External factors such as strikes, weather or government policy may radically alter the picture.

The sensible company approaches risk by recognizing each possible risk area and taking steps to minimize it. For example, delay is a common risk which always costs money as well as time yet adequacy of finance can at least avoid total failure. Once risks have been minimized some attempt should be made to quantify them or at least consider what will happen if the project fails, i.e. what is the downside risk. It is this last item, rather than a sophisticated analysis of return and risk, which may be the deciding factor in considering a project.

It would be incorrect to interpret the previous comments as meaning that high return is only possible when risks are high. Unusually good returns can be obtained in a number of situations where risks may not be excessive such as:

1   A product is unique and protected by patents.
2   Special skill is needed.
3   A company has a monopoly of the market.
4   There is a very high cost of entry to the market.
5   A company has the sole source of supply of the product.

It can be seen that the whole subject of return and risk is complex and seldom are easy answers available from analysis. Despite such analysis the final decision will still depend on management judgement. It is probably true that risk analysis in a numerical sense is almost impossible for a small company but a consideration of the risk areas is not, and should always be made.

3.4.3   *Comparison of Average Returns in Different Industries*

It is interesting to compare the average returns on capital employed which are achieved in different industries.

Table 3.2 illustrates some average rates of return for different industries for the year 1977. Also given is the average net profit margin. It will be seen that the range of rates of returns is quite large, the lowest being 8% for road hauliers and the highest being 44% for electronic component distributors. The range of net profit margins is also great, the lowest being 1% for grocery wholesalers, the highest being 12% for pharmaceutical manufacturers and book publishers.

It would be dangerous to draw general conclusions from these figures. Firstly, only one year is shown and the results can vary widely

Table 3.2 Average Net Profit Margin and Return on Capital in Different Industries in 1977

	Net Profit Margin (%)	Return on Capital (%)
Construction Industry		
Joinery manufacturers	6	11
Builders' merchants	4	15
Plant hire	9	13
Chemicals and Plastics Industry		
Chemicals	9	18
Plastics processors	8	18
Pharmaceutical manufacturers	12	22
Plastic packagings	9	27
Electrical and Electronics Industry		
Electronic component manufacturers	6	12
Domestic appliance manufacturers	4	13
Computer equipment manufacturers	11	22
Electrical wholesalers	3	14
Electronic component distributors	11	44
Metals Industry		
Steel producers	7	13
Metal stockholders	5	16
Engineering Industry		
Mechanical handling	10	25
Machine tool manufacturers	6	11
Engineering distributors	6	19
Food Industry		
Bakers	3	9
Frozen food manufacturers	3	9
Meat processors	4	16
Grocery wholesalers	1	18
Supermarkets	3	17
Motor Industry		
Component manufacturers	8	17
Car dealers	2	10
Publishing Industry		
Newspaper publishers	5	11
Book publishers	12	25
Periodical publishers	10	30
Textile Industry		
Clothing manufacturers	6	20
Carpet manufacturers	4	9
Miscellaneous		
Jewellery manufacturers	11	27
Furniture manufacturers	8	26
Road hauliers	3	8

Abstracted from: Inter-Company Comparisons Ltd. 1977
Industrial Performance Analysis

Profitability

from year to year. Secondly, average figures are given and these hide wide variations. Table 3.3 illustrates this point by giving some results, also for 1977, split between company size and giving some idea of the range within each group. The spread of results is shown by, for example, clothing retailing. At the extreme, rates of return of 93% (upper quartile large companies) and −7% (i.e. losses, lower quartile medium companies).

Table 3.3 Return of Capital (%) Employed in 1977 in Different-sized Companies

	Size of Companies								
	Large			Medium			Small		
	Upper Quartile	Median	Lower Quartile	Upper Quartile	Median	Lower Quartile	Upper Quartile	Median	Lower Quartile
Textile Manufacturers 1977	39	24	10	30	15	8	40	8	0.3
Carpet Manufacturers	28	14	8	28	17	3	27	16	2
Clothing Manufacturers	61	40	10	40	30	16	37	24	1
Clothing Retailing	93	33	8	31	10	−7	35	20	1

Abstracted from: Dun & Bradstreet: Management Ratios

A further point is that net margin and rate of return do not correlate. For example, grocery wholesalers averaged 1% net margin (the lowest result) yet 18% return on capital (an above average result). Such a result is possible when relatively little capital is required (possibly because of advantageous differences in the terms of trade, e.g. credit from suppliers but cash terms on sales). However, a particular danger of a low margin business is that a profit very easily becomes a loss if financial control is not of the highest standard.

3.5 Action Points

1 Define corporate objectives to decide how profitable the business should be.
2 Recognize the difficulties of defining how much profit has been made.
3 Consider productivity as one area for profit improvement.
4 Compare the company's performance with others if suitable statistics are available. It is a useful management control.

IV
Cash Management

4.1 Introduction

Cash is the lifeblood of any business activity but in sophisticated businesses it is easy to forget two things of great importance. First, a principal objective of any business activity is to make a profit and this has no meaning unless the proprietors or shareholders ultimately receive cash payments as dividend and/or sale proceeds from the business. Secondly, a business will survive or fail in the short term on its ability to pay its bills as they fall due. Cash management (as distinct from the more general concept of financial management) is concerned with control of the cash resources of a business with particular emphasis on ensuring there is an adequacy of cash at all times to meet the needs of that business.

The importance of this aspect of management cannot be stressed too strongly. It is a sad fact that many small companies do not pay serious attention to cash planning until crises occur; either it is not considered important or management does not have sufficient time. Even if management does not prepare other information statements, some attempt at cash forecasting should be regarded as essential if unnecessary risks of cash shortage are to be avoided. An alternative is to operate the business with substantial cash reserves at all times but this is normally inefficient, as cash invested in business assets can usually show a greater return than in a bank deposit account.

4.2 Cash Flow

The passage of cash through a business is a two-way flow. Cash from sales receipts is incoming whereas most other cash flow is outgoing and includes payment for supplies, wages, dividends, etc. These flows

Cash Management

are illustrated in Figure 4.1. If incoming cash consistently exceeds outgoing cash, cash balances will build up whereas if the opposite is true the company will either require further cash injections from shareholders/lenders or run out of cash (and become insolvent). Cash management is concerned with achieving a satisfactory and controlled balance between these two flows.

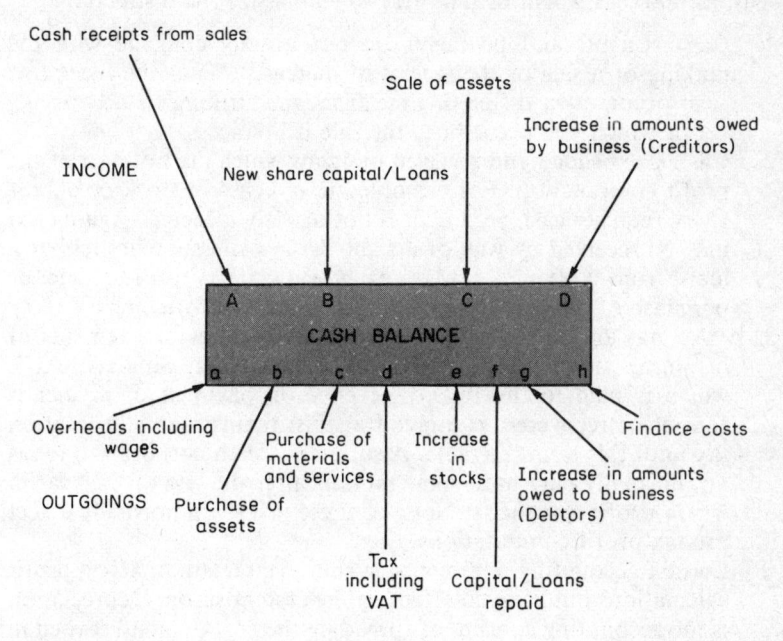

Figure 4.1 The Cash Flows of a Business
Notes

1. Some flows may reverse. For example a decrease in stock levels is a cash input.
2. Cash is increasing if, over the period considered, $A+B+C+D$ is greater than $a+b+c+d+e+f+g+h$ and vice versa.

It must first be recognized that cash flow and profitability are not directly related, indeed paradoxically cash can become tightest when profits are greatest. For example, if turnover is growing fast profits may well be higher than previously. However, cash will become tighter than before if the cash required for the increases in stock and debtors, resulting from the increased level of turnover, is greater than the cash resulting from the corresponding increase in creditors plus the extra profit which is being achieved. This is a common situation and it underlines the need to plan carefully. As a further illustration of the separation between cash and profit, cash balances will often increase as turnover falls (for reasons opposite to those above) yet, in these circumstances, it could hardly be said that the increasing cash balance is an indication of the health of the business. In such a case, the lower turnover is likely to lead to losses which, if not halted, will in time erode the temporarily increased cash balance and lead to insolvency.

Cash flow differs from profitability or profit flow for several reasons and it is worth listing these to emphasize the distinction:

1. Cash receipts and payments do not usually coincide with the making of a sale or the receipt of materials. Thus the receipt of cash occurs at a different time from the striking of accounting profit which will occur once the sale is invoiced.
2. Cash is expended and received on items which are not part of the profit computation. For example, an increase in stock or debtor levels requires cash yet profit is not directly affected. Again cash may be received by way of a rights issue from shareholders or a loan from a bank, neither of which affects profit. Sale or purchase of fixed assets is also a cash, not a profit, item.
3. VAT has an impact on cash flow because dates of payments of incoming and outgoing flows will be different. Similarly ACT which is paid to the Inland Revenue on payment of dividends cannot be recovered as a credit against mainstream corporation tax until this tax is payable. Also, mainstream corporation tax is not normally paid until some months after the end of the year in which profit was made. None of these taxes will normally affect pre-tax profit computations.
4. Certain accounting treatments, such as depreciation, affect profit calculations but have no effect on the cash position. Depreciation is the accounting concept of spreading the cost of an asset used in the business (which has already been incurred and paid) over its useful life, so as not to distort seriously the calculation of profit in the year in which the asset is purchased. In that year cash is expended on the capital item but profit is not greatly affected as only a proportion of the cost will be charged to the profit and loss account.

The differences between cash and profit are highlighted by Tables 4.1 and 4.2 which illustrate corresponding cash flow and profit forecasts. The retained profit of £49,176 contrasts strongly with the summarized cash decrease of £9,550. In comparing these summaries the points to note are as follows:

Included in cash but not profit
Loans receivable   £15,000
Actual tax paid   £17,126

Capital expenditure	£71,000	
Loan repayments	£ 3,000	
Included in profit but not cash		
Stock increase	£20,000	(which is an adjustment of purchases and relevant wages to correspond with sales)
Depreciation	£10,000	
Book value of assets sold	£2,100	
Tax calculated on profits	£25,400	(i.e. not actual tax paid)

4.3 Working Capital

A concept which is widely used in discussions of cash availability (or liquidity) is that of working capital. This is commonly taken as one of three possibilities:

1 current assets (stock, debtors, short term investments, bills receivable, and cash;
2 liquid assets (cash, debtors, and bills receivable);
3 current assets less current liabilities, i.e. net current assets.

The first definition indicates the cash availability if all current assets were converted into cash. The second reflects the fact that stock may be more difficult to turn into cash (as sales must first be made and, if stock includes raw materials, products must be manufactured then sold). The third description is really net cash which would be available if all current assets were converted into cash and all current liabilities paid from the proceeds.

It is not easy to specify how much working capital is necessary to run a business prudently without preparing a full cash flow forecast which will reveal projected changes over time. However, certain rules of thumb are used in assessing businesses which do at least give a preliminary indication. The current ratio (see Table 2.4), i.e. current assets divided by current liabilities, is one such indicator. It is commonly stated that this ratio should be of the order of at least 2:1. However, many soundly run businesses have a lower ratio and further enquiry will always be required before definitive conclusions can be reached. For example, a bank overdraft is strictly speaking a current liability but many companies have overdrafts which include an

Table 4.1 Cash Flow Forecast

	JAN £	FEB £	MAR £	APRIL £	MAY £	JUNE £	JULY £	AUG £	SEPT £	OCT £	NOV £	DEC £	Total £
Receipts													
From debtors	18,500	18,500	19,000	19,000	19,000	19,000	20,000	20,000	13,000	20,500	21,000	21,000	228,500
Other income			825			825			825			825	3,300
Realization of assets			1,000		2,000	1,000							4,000
Loans receivable			15,000										15,000
A Total	18,500	18,500	35,825	19,000	21,000	20,825	20,000	20,000	13,825	20,500	21,000	21,825	250,800
Payments													
For purchases & services	7,000	7,000	7,500	8,000	8,000	8,500	9,000	9,000	9,000	6,000	9,500	9,500	98,000
Wages, salaries, etc.	4,900	4,900	5,500	5,500	5,500	5,500	5,500	2,500	6,500	6,500	6,500	6,500	65,800
Taxation	17,126												17,126
Dividends (net)							1,762					1,762	3,524
Capital expenditure		5,000	10,000	5,000	10,000	40,000			1,500		1,000		71,000
Loan repayments			1,500						900				3,000
Loan interest			900										1,800
B Total	29,026	16,900	25,400	18,500	23,500	54,000	16,262	11,500	17,900	12,500	17,000	17,762	260,250
C (= A − B) Excess (deficiency) of receipts over payments	(10,526)	1,600	10,425	500	(2,500)	(33,175)	3,738	8,500	(4,075)	8,000	4,000	4,063	(9,550)
D Cash Balance (overdraft) at start	10,875	349	1,949	12,374	12,874	10,374	(22,801)	(19,063)	(10,563)	(14,638)	(6,638)	(2,638)	(1,425)
E (= D + C) Cash Balance (overdraft) at end	349	1,949	12,374	12,874	10,374	(22,801)	(19,063)	(10,563)	(14,638)	(6,638)	(2,638)	(1,425)	(10,975)

Note: The items of income and expenditure have been summarized for purposes of illustration. In particular VAT (both an incoming and outgoing flow) has been omitted.

Table 4.2 Profit Forecast Equivalent of Table 4.1

Profit for the whole year (compare with cash flow forecast totals)

Sales		228,500
Other Income		3,300
		231,800
Purchases, etc.	98,000	
Wages, etc.	65,800	
Opening Stock 151,000		
Closing Stock 171,000		
	(20,000)	
		143,800
		88,000
Loan interest	1,800	
Depreciation	10,000	
		11,800
Pre-tax profit on trading		76,200
Profit on sale of assets:		
Proceeds of sale	4,000	
Less: Book value	2,100	
		1,900
Pre-tax profit		78,100
Less: *Taxation*		25,400
Profit after tax		52,700
Less: *Dividends*		3,524
Profit retained		£49,176

element of longer-term asset financing at a particular time and this will artificially depress the ratio. Again the acid test, i.e. current assets excluding stock divided by current liabilities, is normally expected to exceed 1:1. Thus the receipts of payments from debtors plus any cash in hand would be sufficient to pay all creditors. However, a cash business may be soundly run with almost no debtors (but probably much stock) and many creditors (reflecting the purchase of stock). In such a case the ratio would be much less than one.

It is most important to estimate the future working capital needs of a business if potential crises are to be avoided. It is possible to reach an approximate conclusion by estimating future stocks, debtors, and creditors from a forecast of sales levels. Arithmetically stock increase plus debtor increase minus creditor increase will give a figure for

Managing Your Company's Finances

working capital increase (which must be provided by retained profit, share subscription and/or borrowing). Unfortunately, such an answer can be dangerously misleading, as it ignores timing, and there is no satisfactory alternative to a properly prepared cash flow.

4.4 Cash Flow Forecasting

The introduction of cash forecasting is probably the most effective way of strengthening financial control in a business which has formerly done no proper management accounting.

At its simplest a cash forecast estimates the amounts of cash to be received and expended in a particular period, the net effect of which is to increase (or decrease) the cash balance carried forward into the next period. Frequently the period chosen will be one month (because many accounts are charged and paid monthly) and the forecast will extend over six months to a year. The vital information to be obtained from this forecast is whether the company can exist throughout the forecast periods within its existing cash and/or borrowing resources. If not steps must be taken to reduce cash needs or raise more money.

The key to the preparation of such a forecast is not only to estimate, accurately, income and overheads (as is done for a profit forecast) but also to estimate the timing of such receipts and payments. It can be appreciated that the assumptions contained in a profit forecast will also apply to the equivalent cash forecast but additional assumptions concerning timing must be made. The large number of assumptions can make a cash forecast particularly difficult to prepare accurately but its value more than outweighs the work required. The uncertainties involved also mean that the forecast becomes less reliable as it attempts to predict further into the future. It is thus important to note that any cash flow will need periodic revision. For example, a company might prepare a revised twelve month forecast every three months (a 'rolling forecast').

Table 4.1 gives a simple example to illustrate the principles involved. It has been prepared by listing each item of income and expenditure in detail at the time it is forecast to occur and summarizing the totals under each heading as shown.

Taking, for example, the month of January the company is forecasting to receive £18,500 (A) (probably from sales made in, say, November) and to pay out £20,026 (B) (some of which will relate to purchases made in, say, November), resulting in a net figure of £10,526 (C) paid out. Thus the cash balance of £10,875 (D) at the beginning of the month is forecast to reduce to £349 (E) by the end of the month. This figure (E) becomes the opening cash balance for the

Cash management

next month (D). The bottom line of the forecast (E) shows the cumulative effect of the increase or decrease in cash balances forecast for each month in turn. It can be directly compared with the total of cash and borrowing resources to see if action is required.

Several important points about the preparation of such a forecast need consideration:

1. The whole cash flow is dependent on a properly prepared sales forecast from which the majority of the income forecast is derived.
2. Having made a month by month sales forecast a realistic assumption about the amount of credit taken by customers must be made, i.e. how long will it be from invoicing to the date of payment? (Historical performance is a good preliminary guide).
3. From the sales forecast a reasonable estimate of purchases to achieve the required level of output can usually be made. Again, the credit period is important.
4. Certain items such as rates, rent, wages may be easy to estimate, but inflationary or other increases must not be overlooked.
5. It is normally prudent not to allow for uncertain income (a disputed debt for instance) but to allow for all possible expenditure. In this respect some over-estimate of the time customers take to pay and some under-estimate of the time the company takes to pay will give a more prudent picture than the reverse.
6. In periods which show a heavy use of bank overdraft facilities, for example, it may be necessary to examine the cash flow more closely on, say, a week-by-week basis particularly if outgoing and incoming payments are especially large.

Having prepared the cash flow it is reasonable to enquire not only whether it is sufficiently conservative but also how sensitive it is to errors in the assumptions. For example, if the sales forecast is in doubt because of the absence of firm orders it is sensible to prepare a 'worst case' forecast as well as a 'most likely out-turn' forecast and to examine the sensitivity of the cash flow (and resulting overdraft) to this possibility. Other sensitivities may need to be examined if, for example, the inflation rate is hard to predict or terms of trade in the industry are volatile. All of this work better prepares management for what is at best an uncertain future and it may mean that plans can be made to mitigate certain potentially dangerous changes should these occur. It is probably true that the more carefully management has considered future possible difficulties before they happen and the alternative actions to take, the better able they will be to cope if the need arises. For example, if the forecast indicates cash will become tight due to a worsening trading climate, management can decide to protect the cash position by deferring certain non-essential items of expenditure such as fixed asset replacement.

A sample blank form cash flow forecast is given in Table 4.4 (equivalent to Table 4.1). In use it will require detailed schedules to be attached.

4.5 Sources and Applications of Funds Statements

A cash flow forecast indicates what is happening to a company's cash position over a period of time. However, although it does show where the cash has come from or gone to, it does not usually provide an easily digested summary. A statement which does show this is a sources and application of funds statement which is a legal requirement of published accounts (no cash flow being required). Such a statement summarizes the overall change in the items of the balance sheet from one accounting date to another (monthly or yearly) all of which will have involved a change in the cash position. Table 4.3 gives a simple example of this.

Table 4.3 Source and Application of Funds

	This Period £	This Year to date £	Last Year to date £
Source			
Net profit for period	1,500	20,000	15,000
Depreciation for period	500	7,000	5,000
Sale of assets	3,000	3,000	–
Increase in creditors	600	1,200	1,000
Loan capital/share issues	20,000	20,000	–
Total (A)	£25,600	£51,200	£21,000
Application			
Dividends paid (net)	100	100	100
Taxation	–	5,000	4,000
Repayment of loans	1,000	2,000	500
Purchase of assets	25,000	25,000	–
Increase in stocks	1,000	3,000	2,000
Increase in debtors	1,500	4,000	3,000
Total (B)	£28,600	£39,100	£9,600
Net Increase (Decrease) in Cash Position (A – B)	(£3,000)	£12,100	£11,400

Table 4.4 Cash Flow Forecast

Period	1 £	2 £	3 £	4 £	5 £	6 £	7 £	8 £	9 £	10 £	11 £	12 £	Total £
Receipts													
From debtors													
Other income													
Realization of assets													
Loans receivable													
VAT													
A *Total*													
Payments													
For purchases & services													
Wages, salaries, etc.													
Taxation													
Dividend (net)													
Capital expenditure													
Loan repayments													
Loan interest													
VAT													
B *Total*													
C (= A − B) *Excess (deficiency) of receipts over payments*													
D *Balance (overdraft) at start*													
E (= D + C) *Balance (overdraft) at end*													

Managing Your Company's Finances

The value of the statement is that it summarizes the use to which net income has been employed in the period concerned. It is, however, in reality nothing more than a summarized historic (rather than forecast) cash flow statement presented in a particular way. Such statements are sometimes prepared showing changes in working capital rather than cash which means that current asset changes are omitted from the sources and applications summary and thus remain in the net total figure, which then becomes an increase or decrease in working capital.

4.6 Management of a Cash Surplus

From time to time most companies have cash surplus to their immediate requirements. Large public companies have employees in their treasurer's departments who are skilled in the deployment of such funds to maximum advantage but the smaller company often gives little thought to cash management in this sense. However, cash surpluses can earn valuable revenue if a little care is taken.

There are three distinct categories of cash surplus, namely:

1. Very short term swings in the company's overdraft position resulting in a credit balance.
2. Periods of a week or two to several months when the company has cash surpluses.
3. Semi-permanent cash balances which tend to grow as profit is made.

These categories will be considered in turn. The first category is what a bank hopes to see when an overdraft facility is provided, i.e. the current account balance swings within, say, a month between overdraft and credit. In such cases credit balances last for brief periods and little can be done to earn revenue on such balances as UK banks do not normally pay interest on current account balances. If the amounts are substantial and the company can afford the time and effort even short term credit balances can, through a bank for example, be put out on the money market. Unfortunately, this requires accurate knowledge of the pattern of the account balance and it is probably uneconomic in a small company.

Cash balances which remain for a period of weeks or months are another matter. There are a number of ways such balances can earn interest:

1. A bank deposit account which pays gross interest, i.e. no tax is deducted. Notice of withdrawal may be required.
2. A building society account. Interest will be paid net of basic rate income tax and notice of withdrawal will be required if amounts invested are substantial.

3 Money market. Most banks will put customers' money out on the money market (provided amounts are at least, say, tens of thousands of pounds) and will offer rates which reflect the rate the bank itself will obtain. Such deposits can range from overnight to one year with three month and six month deposits being particularly common. Generally speaking, longer-term deposits will earn higher rates of interest than shorter ones but the commitment is absolute. In other words, the money will not be repayable until the end of the contracted period and thus good forecasting of cash needs is essential.

Cash balances which remain almost permanently in a company's balance sheet involve different considerations from the other cases discussed. It is worth considering what purposes such balances serve and specific policy should be agreed. If a company is successful it should be able to obtain higher returns on capital invested in its business than on cash on deposit. Thus it can be argued that whilst cash does indicate strength it also indicates a lack of efficiency in the use of resources leading to a reduction in the return shareholders could otherwise achieve.

The options open to a company with substantial cash balances can be summarized as follows:

1 Can the company find worthwhile scope for further investment in its existing business, e.g. new premises or new plant?
2 Can the company find worthwhile investment opportunities in other businesses? This might involve acquisitions or new projects.
3 If neither of these two is attractive, one option is to pay the cash to shareholders by way of dividend (or salary bonus in proprietor managed companies). Until recently, this was unattractive because of the very high tax rates involved but the option may be attractive at lower tax rates. Alternatively, the company may decide to retain the cash for future investment possibilities in which case similar considerations to those required for shorter term balances are necessary in the meantime. Thus a careful cash forecast will be required and a list of options as to where to put the cash, the repayment constraints applying and the interest rate for each possibility. If balances are substantial it will probably be prudent to spread the cash around various deposit takers and to include a range of maturities, both to match forecast needs and to provide some flexibility.

4.7 Action Points

1 Prepare cash flow forecasts. The introduction of cash flow

Managing Your Company's Finances

forecasting is the most effective way of strengthening financial control.
2 Note there is a big difference between cash and profit.
3 Consider the management of cash surpluses when these occur to improve the return to shareholders.

V
Credit Control (Sales)

5.1 Introduction

The previous chapter discussed cash management in the sense of planning and forecasting. This chapter and the next are concerned with an equally important aspect of overall cash control, that is, making sure debts are collected and settled properly. This aspect of financial management is usually known as credit control.

This chapter is about the control and collection of the company's debtors which will mostly comprise sales invoices. Just as the importance of overall cash management has been stressed in maximizing financial returns on the one hand and ensuring survival on the other, so it can be argued that credit control of sales is crucial to the achievement of these objectives. Many companies who find themselves in financial difficulties do so because they are incurring bad debts (i.e. credit risk assessment is poor) and/or are failing to collect money due on time (i.e. collection is poor). This discipline demands close attention in even the smallest company and an information system which tells management how well the credit control is working is essential in all but the simplest businesses.

5.2 The Nature of Credit Control

The nature of the credit control system will depend on the type of industry in which the company operates. Three broad categories are worth considering separately:

1. A cash business where all revenue is received in cash or its equivalent at the time of sale. This includes retailing, restaurant operation and much mail order.
2. A sales invoice business where credit is normally given and thus

Managing Your Company's Finances

sales revenue is not received until some time after the sale is made. Most manufacturers and wholesalers operate in this way.
3   A contracting business where work is done over an extended period of time and revenue is usually received at agreed points along the contract rather than all on completion. Specialist manufacturers (doing one-off jobs) and builders operate in this manner.

5.2.1   Cash Business

In one sense credit control of sales is not required as no credit is given, i.e. the goods do not exchange hands unless cash is paid to the seller. However, the practical situation is not quite so simple. Firstly, it is common practice nowadays for most retailers to accept cheques and possibly credit cards in payment for goods. Any retailer who does not is risking a loss of trade but the receipt of money in this way involves credit control because of the risk that cheques are not valid or credit cards are stolen.

The clearing bank cheque cards have done much to protect retailers from bouncing cheques but the recipient of the cheque must properly follow the bank's instructions if the cheque is to be honoured in the event of difficulty and such cards do only guarantee cheques up to a specified limit. This involves training staff to make the proper checks and the possibility of human error will remain. The same general comments about care in operating the system applies to credit cards. Expiry dates and signatures must be checked and, if the amount to be charged to the card exceeds a specified figure, it is necessary to telephone the credit card company's control office for sanction. Again there is ample scope for human error.

Provided payment is received in a satisfactory manner it would be tempting to believe all is well. Unfortunately cash businesses are notorious for staff theft. If all sales are accompanied by a receipt, a numbered copy of which remains in the company's records, there is little risk, but many businesses do not have such a system and the avoidance of loss of cash by theft needs careful attention.

5.2.2   Sales Invoice Business

This general system is common throughout industrial and commercial life. The problems can be readily summarized:

1   Is the customer credit worthy?
2   Are payments being received from customers on the agreed dates?
3   Are there frequent disputes over the amount owing due to poor preparation of invoices?

Credit Control (Sales)

4   Are there frequent disputes over the quality of goods resulting in contested situations and non-payment?

The fourth of these questions, though important, is not a credit control problem at all but rather a fault of production or sales if the customer has been misled or wrongly supplied. The others are of vital importance to the credit controller and need constant attention and monitoring.

5.2.3   Contracting Business

The main credit control problems of the sales invoice situation also arise here but the relationship with the customer in connection with one sale lasts so much longer that other problems can occur. It is important to establish at the outset what is to be the payment basis – which may differ somewhat from contract to contract. Not only may the frequency of payments be important but the amounts may differ from the original estimate because of, for example, an agreed basis of charging for price increases in material or labour costs. Thus it is important to specify all such details in the original agreement if disputes are not to arise. Provided this is properly done the job of credit control is very similar to a sales invoice business and the emphasis falls on debt collection once the agreed periodic invoices are issued.

5.3   Operating a Credit Control System

5.3.1   Cash Business

Good credit control depends on establishing a proper system with the object of ensuring staff are aware of what is required and that performance can be satisfactorily and constantly monitored.

In a cash business it is normal practise to require all cheque and credit card business to be overseen by certain authorized members of staff. This has the object of reducing human error which will tend to be higher with young and inexperienced staff. Even then some errors will inevitably occur and loss will result. Monitoring is, however, fairly straightforward as losses can be compared with either total sales or, better, with cheque or credit card sales. This ratio will, if examined frequently, give a good indication of whether corrective action is required.

The more difficult problem can be staff theft of cash. Stock may also be stolen but this is a stock control rather than credit control problem. As mentioned above, if all sales are accompanied by a

Managing Your Company's Finances

receipt control is easier as cash balances can easily and frequently (probably daily) be checked against receipts totals and the only difference should be the occasional human error. The best of modern cash tills incorporate security measures to make staff theft more difficult and a careful study of the types available before purchase is worthwhile.

It usually makes sense wherever possible to make one member of staff responsible for handling cash collection. This makes theft more difficult as the prime suspect is immediately obvious. Where this is not practicable it is necessary to compare suitable ratios over a period of time. One of these may, for example, be net profit margin on turnover which has the merit of indicating any theft whether of goods or cash. Ironically, this is often more effective in a bigger business with many outlets when detailed comparisons of performance between different branches can be made and worrying variances are more apparent. It is the cash business with only two or three outlets that can be most at risk in the sense that theft is not quickly spotted. The single outlet business is usually fairly secure because of the proprietor's constant presence.

5.3.2 Sales Invoice Business

Here the credit control system will be primarily concerned with two areas, namely establishing credit limits for particular customers and ensuring invoices are settled on time.

When a new customer comes along, the first job of the credit controller is to decide whether he is credit worthy. Unless much is already known about him it is always prudent to run a credit check. Provided the customer is a limited company, it is easy to do a search at Companies House and obtain recently filed accounts which give some indication of financial strength. Certain organizations, such as Dun and Bradstreet Ltd. and U.A.P.T., specialize in doing such searches on behalf of clients and making other enquiries which may expose credit risks. References can also be sought from other credit suppliers of the new customer to see whether payments are usually made promptly. Having made such checks it is prudent to limit total initial credit invoices to a fairly low level until experience of the customer's promptness of payment has been established. If there are real doubts it may be necessary to ask for payment without credit for a period and gradually move to credit terms if all goes well. The effectiveness of the company's credit checks can be monitored by comparing bad debts with turnover. Table 5.1 gives an example of a blank creditor proposal report to the board.

In certain cases it may be worth considering credit risk insurance.

Credit Control (Sales)

Table 5.1 Credit Account Proposals

New Account Requests

Name	Search Results					References	Proposed Initial Limit
	Year	Net Profit	Net Assets	Borrowings	Notes		

Proposed Increases

Name	Search Results					Experience and Comments	Existing Limit	Proposed New Limit
	Year	Net Profit	Net Assets	Borrowings	Notes			

For example, ECGD provides a very full cover of the credit risks associated with exporting when political risks, for example, can be a major worry. Besides applying initial credit limits to new customers because of doubts about their credit worthiness and reliability, it is also prudent to consider whether any customer should be allowed so much credit that, if the customer failed and the debt became bad, the company's own existence would be threatened. A small and young company may have to accept such risks as part and parcel of establishing itself but the opportunity should always be sought to minimize this type of exposure as soon as possible.

Once credit invoices have been issued, the main task of credit control is to ensure debts are paid on time. It is common experience that many companies take as much credit as they can regardless of the agreed terms of trade and thus will not pay on time unless chased. A control system depends on frequently producing a list of overdue debtors. Such a list is usually aged, i.e. grouping the debtors in settlement date order. The list can then be used to chase the offenders. It can also be used to monitor credit control performance by comparing, for example, overdue debtors with total debtors. Tables 5.2 and 5.3 give examples of blank reports to the company's board on these points.

Table 5.2   Aged Debtor List

Company Name	Credit Limit	Total Outstanding	Current	Over 30 days	Over 60 days	Notes/Proposals for Action
TOTAL		(100%)	(%)	(%)	(%)	Average Debtor Period = days
Same Period Last Year		(100%)	(%)	(%)	(%)	Average Debtor Period = days

Credit Control (Sales)

Many credit control problems centre around minor disagreements over the amount due. It is always advisable to send out monthly statements summarizing amounts owing for goods supplied less amounts received. This summary usually overcomes many of the excuses for slow payment which arise from invoices alone.

When chasing debts it is usually more effective to use the telephone than a letter if the customer list is short enough for this to be practicable. Not only is the telephone a quicker means of communication but the personal contact is generally beneficial. If customers persist in not paying despite reminders the company must

Table 5.3 Overdue and Problem Accounts

1 *Difficult and Slow*

	This Period	% Total	Same Period Last Year	%
Unpaid (no specific reason)				
Disputed invoice/statement				
2 *Bad Debt Performance*				
Actual bad debts				
Suspected bad debts				
Total				

3 *Breakdown of Suspected Bad Debts and Serious Problems*

Name	Credit Limit	Amount Outstanding	Average Period Outstanding	Action Taken	Notes/ Proposals

Managing Your Company's Finances

consider sanctions such as legal action and withholding supplies. The latter action is often the most powerful as it is both cheap and efficient provided the customer needs the supplies and cannot easily get them elsewhere.

Unfortunately, big companies are often the worst offenders when it comes to extended payment delays. Sometimes the product supplied is important and the non-supply sanction works but, generally, it is vital not to become too dependent on one big company account or advantage can, and often will, be taken of this dependence. Also it must be recognized that big organizations can be hard to deal with because of, for example, difficulties in tracing the man responsible. Commonly, small companies tend to be too readily overawed by big customers and, therefore, not to chase debts with enough fervour because of the assumed (or actual) importance of the account.

5.3.3 Contracting Business

The comments of the previous paragraph apply equally well to contracting. However, as the work done will be paid for by a series of invoices it becomes important to have a system to produce invoices at the earliest possible opportunity once the agreed invoice point is reached. Such invoices often depend on an independent expert's verification of the value of work done since the last invoice, and he needs clear instructions on what is required. With long contracts it is always sensible to have progress charts which are kept up to date. These charts can compare physical progress with expectation and can also incorporate the cash receipt performance. Table 5.4 gives a simple example of a blank report to the board.

As with normal sales invoice business, payments may well have to be chased to achieve consistently good cash receipts. In case of difficulties the sanction of refusing to continue can sometimes not be readily usable as the company's own staff and other resources may be committed to the contract so that they would become idle if work ceased and losses would ensue. This heavy dependence on the customer continuing to pay means that a thorough check on credit-worthiness before work commences is even more important than in a sales invoice situation. Indeed, many engineering contracts now specify that, say, one-third of the payment is received in advance of work commencing.

A final point to note is that many contracts have an element of retainer. In other words the customer retains 5% or 10% of the bill until he is satisfied the work has been completed satisfactorily. Disputes are common at this stage and it must not be forgotten that the retainer is probably equivalent to the net profit margin on the job and that the longer it takes to receive the money the less valuable it is. Thus the company must concentrate on finishing its contracts properly without loose ends and the credit controller must ensure retainers are not held back unnecessarily.

5.4 Discounts

It is common in some industries to offer a discount for cash on early settlement of invoices. This is sometimes used to ease debt collection and sometimes used to obtain shorter average debtor life than is normal in the industry because of tight liquidity.

The true cost of offering discounts should be always considered. For example, a 2.5% discount for settling a debt 30 days earlier than otherwise equates to an annualized interest rate of 30%. Thus, provided the company has the borrowing capacity and interest rates on its overdraft are less than 30%, it would be beneficial not to offer discounts and to accept the longer credit period by making greater use of bank facilities at the ruling interest rate. It will be appreciated that annualized interest rate equivalents of even quite small discounts can be very high indeed. There are, of course, circumstances where cash is so tight and borrowing power is exhausted that debts must be collected as soon as possible and at whatever cost. In all other circumstances, however, the relative cost of offering discounts should be balanced against whatever other advantage there might seem to be.

Discounts are also commonly offered for bulk supply of goods compared with the price for limited numbers. It is tempting to offer large discounts to increase turnover but the exercise should be properly costed. The key to such costing is that the company should be better off in profit terms in selling more goods at a discount than a small number at no discount. Cost savings in invoicing, delivery and packing for example are real and a sensible discount structure can be worthwhile but it is unwise to adopt such a structure without a costing exercise first just because a competitor does so.

5.5 The Importance of Control

This is such an important topic that it is worth summarizing and supplementing the relevant control points that have already been made as well as considering ways of dealing with difficult debts.

A. *When giving new credit accounts it is prudent to:*

1   do a company search;
2   take trade references;

Managing Your Company's Finances

3   not allow high levels of credit until some experience of the account has been gained;
4   consider credit insurance where appropriate.

B. *General points on credit accounts:*

1   send out regular statements to minimize the excuses for delay for petty reasons;
2   ensure the system always produces an invoice when goods or services are supplied;
3   try and avoid any debtor becoming so large that major difficulties (delay or insolvency) could cause survival problems for the company;
4   all debtors will need chasing from time to time. Some only need reminding initially that the company likes to see payment on time, others will require constant reminding;
5   chasing by personal contact (e.g. telephone) is usually more effective than by letter.

C. *How to deal with really difficult payers:*

1   withhold supplies until the account is brought up to date;
2   a personal visit by a member of staff may be sufficiently embarrassing or aggravating to produce a cheque. Such cheques also have the merit that they do not get lost in the post;
3   if the difficulties are due to real cash problems of the customer it may be sensible to negotiate extended payment terms rather than see the customer fail and almost certainly receive nothing. Small weekly payments are one possibility – perhaps on standing order;
4   a demand for payment or a writ can be served through a solicitor if the debt remains unpaid. This process involves court judgements and costs and may eventually lead to a petition for winding up the customer company. It is drastic action. It will succeed if the customer is just refusing to pay. If he is genuinely unable to pay, a liquidation will almost certainly result and recovery of money is unlikely, as secured and preferential creditors will probably absorb all proceeds.
5   early warnings of customer problems should always be looked for. A change in the payment behaviour leading to progressively increasing difficulties is one such sign. Another useful source of information is salesmen who visit the customers' premises and will often notice things of value to the credit controller if they are encouraged to report back.

Credit Control (Sales)

These points emphasize the need for frequent monitoring of the performance of the credit control system. The performance statistics should be regularly considered by the board and all statistics should be compared with previous performance to highlight adverse changes. These monitoring statistics should include:

1. An aged list of debtors containing comparisons with previous experience. A calculation of average debtor period is useful for comparison purposes. Table 5.1 gives an example of a simple blank report.
2. A schedule of problem accounts with notes and proposals for action. Table 5.2 gives an example of a suitable blank report.
3. A summary of bad debt performance compared with previous experience. See Table 5.2.
4. Proposals for credit limits on any very large new or politically risky account. Table 5.3 gives an example of a suitable blank report.

5.6 Action Points

1. Introduce a proper credit control system.
2. Monitor performance of the system with suitable statistics regularly presented to top management.
3. Be alert to adverse changes including the payment performance of particular customers who may become the next bad debt.
4. Always check credit worthiness before supplying on credit terms.
5. Be aware of the advantages and disadvantages of discounts.

Table 5.4 Contracting Schedule

Name	Job No.	Total Quote	Payment Basis	Invoiced to Date	Collected to Date	Average Payment Period	Comments
TOTALS							

VI
Credit Control (Purchases)

6.1 Introduction

The content of this chapter is closely related to that of the previous chapter but here it is the outgoing cash being paid for purchases (which include for this purpose tax, rent, rates, etc.), rather than the incoming cash from sales, which is of interest. The point was made in chapter 5, and is repeated elsewhere in the book because of its importance, that companies generally do not fail because they are making losses but because they can no longer pay their bills. Inadequate debt collection and/or bad debts are major causes of cash shortage but it is the creditors who will force the actual collapse. If the creditor is a secured lender such as a bank, receivership will probably ensue. Other creditors (who particularly include the Inland Revenue) will precipitate collapse by serving writs leading to a liquidation. So the control of creditors is as important as control of debtors.

6.2 Selecting Suppliers

The company will have little control over creditors such as the Inland Revenue, PAYE, VAT and rates. There will normally be little or no scope for negotiating the terms of credit with such bodies. Certain other overheads such as rent are similar. Here there may be scope for some negotiation before a lease is signed but once completed a lease is seldom easy to change. With such creditors there will be specified dates for payment and while, ideally, such payments should be made on time, a company can usually get away with taking some extra credit when money is tight. Care is needed, however, as such creditors can be amongst the toughest in taking action to recover the debt.

The major creditor area where there is scope for negotiation and need for control is that of purchases. First, excessive uncontrolled purchasing leads to unnecessarily high stocks which have an effect on profit (through the cost of the extra overdraft and storage space required) and, more importantly, a large effect on liquidity. Like failure to collect debtors on time, excessive stocks are a major contributor to insolvency. Thus it is necessary to control the amount of purchases as part of the overall cash management and credit control system. This will involve budgeting, which is the subject of another chapter, and only authorizing certain individuals to place orders. There will be times, however, when it may be necessary to order amounts greater than required because of supply difficulties, or it may be advantageous to do so because the cost saving per unit of bulk purchases is greater than the stocking cost.

Once desired purchasing levels have been established, orders can be placed with selected suppliers. There are several factors to take into account when selecting suppliers. These are:

1 Are the products reliably of the required quality?
2 Are the products always available in the quantities required?
3 Can delivery reliably be made on the agreed dates?
4 How far in advance of delivery must an order be placed?
5 How much credit will the supplier give?
6 What is the price of the products in the required quantities and on the required dates compared to that of competitors?

There is no easy answer to the question of which of these factors is most important. Much will depend on the particular circumstances and there may be a very limited choice of suppliers of certain items. However, reliability of supply at acceptable quality does often dominate as the cost to a company of production hold-ups due to shortages can be enormous. Assuming several possible suppliers exist, all the factors should be considered and a decision taken in the light of these and the company's own constraints including cash resources. Table 6.1 gives a sample blank report to the board on alternative suppliers.

6.3 Terms of Credit

Terms of credit will depend largely on the common practice ruling in the industry at the time but negotiation can be as important, as with price. It should not be forgotten that credit terms and price are related. In other words, provided cash is not short, it may be worthwhile taking little or no credit if the price is advantageously lower.

In considering offering credit terms the supplier is likely to go through a process similar to that described in Section 5.3 (which

Table 6.1 Supplier Proposals for (Product)

Name	Quality	Availability	Order Period	Credit Offered	Price	Discounts
Proposed Choice						

should be re-read in the current context). Thus, the company's established credit rating as evidenced by its accounts and its past standard of treatment of other suppliers will be important. Also the terms of credit may well be, say, sixty days but subject to an overriding limit on the total amount outstanding at any one time. Many good companies benefit in their relationship with suppliers by sending copies of the latest audited accounts to the suppliers as soon as they are published. Not only does this save the supplier doing searches but it suggests there is nothing to hide and, if the accounts show an improvement on the previous year, this may lead to a quick and easy raising of the previous credit limit. Finally, there is nothing more beneficial in developing a good relationship with a supplier than paying his bills on time. Indeed, this may ensure continuity of supply when shortages exist as the supplier is likely to treat his good payers most favourably.

If a supplier is to conduct a contract over a period of time the situation is somewhat more complex than for a normal supplier and the points mentioned in paragraph 5.3.3 need consideration. In addition, if there are doubts about the supplier's ability to fulfil his contract performance, bonds or guarantees may be requested to cover the risks of his failure.

6.4 Control of Payments to Suppliers

A proper system to control outgoing payments is as important as the control of incoming payments. Control points which the system should have include the following:

1. No invoice will be considered for payment until the department receiving the product is satisfied with delivery and commissioning (where appropriate).
2. Payment should preferably be made only against suppliers' statements, not against individual invoices.
3. The suppliers' statements should be reconciled with the received invoices before payment is made.
4. A payment policy should be agreed by the board to cover such matters as the taking of discounts and whether payment should be made before, on or after the due date.
5. Any need to delay payments due to cash difficulties should involve board consideration of which payments to delay and how to deal with the suppliers' credit controllers.

As with control of debtors, relevant statistics should be prepared for regular consideration by the board. These statistics need to include

Credit Control (Purchases)

Table 6.2 Aged Creditor List

Name	Credit Limit	Total Outstanding	Current	Over 30 Days	Over 60 Days	Notes
TOTAL		(100%)	(%)	(%)	(%)	Average Creditor Period = ___ days
Same Period Last Year		(100%)	(%)	(%)	(%)	And for Last Year

average credit period compared both with past performance and the stated credit period. Table 5.2 is an example of such a blank report to the board. If cash is tight proper proposals for dealing with this, in terms of which creditors to extend and how, need to be presented.

6.5 Discounts

Section 5.5 discusses discounts from the point of view of the supplier. Exactly the same logic will apply to the customer. Thus if a supplier is foolish enough to offer a 5% discount for settlement within seven days rather than sixty days this should always be taken if cash is not an overriding factor, as it equates to an equivalent annualized interest rate of 41%.

6.6 Surviving Difficult Times

There is no doubt that it is possible to survive difficult times by not paying creditors on time. Most companies 'stretch' their creditors a little from time to time and companies in serious difficulties have no choice. Provided cash difficulties do not become too severe or last for too long, this is one of the ways of preserving some liquidity to pay

Managing Your Company's Finances

bills which will not wait under any circumstances. The wage bill, for example, will never wait and inability to pay it without extra bank overdraft is often the actual difficulty which precipitates the appointment of a receiver by a bank.

The problem with not paying creditors on time is that it generates ill-will, it may involve withholding of further supplies and it may result in writs. If liquidity is extremely tight the trick is to hold non-essential creditors at bay whilst paying enough to crucial suppliers to keep supplies flowing, and to creditors who might otherwise serve writs without caring about the consequences.

If large arrears of creditors have built up it may be possible to reach agreement to pay these over an extended period of time, all creditors being likely to prefer a small steady stream of payment to nothing. Even the Inland Revenue can sometimes be persuaded to do a deal though all official bodies such as this need to be treated with extreme caution as they will not always be sympathetic to problems (whereas most trade suppliers will) and may not worry unduly about losses on a wind-up. Indeed as certain amounts of tax, for example, will be paid out preferentially to other unsecured and floating charge creditors their loss may not be as great as a normal unsecured creditor's. As a general rule it may be preferable to pay everybody something with explanations rather than leave some completely unpaid and risk writs. Using delayed payment to creditors to survive cash crises can, therefore, certainly work. However, it involves a great deal of time being spent in explaining and arguing with suppliers' credit controllers and may permanently damage the company's standing in the industry. It is not, therefore, to be recommended unless absolutely necessary and the need should never be allowed to arise merely from bad cash forecasting.

Much of the ability to survive tight cash flow depends on the company's having contingency plans and the ability, through proper forecasting, to spot severe trouble before it arrives thus giving time for remedial action. Such action might include selling certain assets which might, for example, include stock sold at heavy discount (and thus a loss) just to raise cash. However, in the final analysis it is often the management's tenacity which matters most. Such periods always lead to considerable strain and hard work and the management must have the ability to cope with this if the problems are prolonged.

One example of considerable survival skill we have seen is a capital goods manufacturer who was heavily insolvent at one point and succeeded in being 18 months in arrears with his PAYE payments to the Inland Revenue. Far from the Revenue forcing liquidation, the customer actually persuaded the Inspector to take him out to lunch to discuss a deal. The company survived.

Credit Control (Purchases)

6.7 Action Points

1. Select suppliers carefully, recognizing the many factors relevant to the decision.
2. Control the level of purchases, including capital expenditure, by budgeting.
3. Terms of trade can be negotiable and relate to price.
4. A good relationship should be developed with suppliers; it is important in difficult times.
5. Implement and regularly monitor a proper control system.

VII
Budgetary Control

This and the next three chapters consider the importance of budgeting and the approach to the design of simple budget systems.

7.1 The Importance of Budgeting

In the very early days of a new business, survival is the key. Nevertheless, even at this early stage some planning and strategy are essential. Earlier chapters have dealt mainly with the analysis of historic accounting information by analysing the results of trading in the past year or more and by interpreting balance sheets which tell something about the present condition of the business. What is not available is information about the future. The future is vitally important. To reach a healthy balance sheet in a year's time needs planning. Sales need selling, products need producing and the control of all activities needs an administration facility. Instant decisions, which were possible in the very early days, cease to be a practical way to ensure growth. The business may be:

1 Moving into new markets which can necessitate the hiring of more salesmen or different types of salesmen.
2 Developing new products. Pricing in a single product company is relatively straightforward. Pricing a range of products needs the discipline of budgeting.
3 Increasing the level, range and complexity of production which may mean new production facilities, methods and costs.
4 Changing the quantity of raw materials, work in progress and finished goods held in stock to facilitate smooth production. This will call for good purchasing and stock control systems and possibly increased storage space.
5 Outgrowing its initial capital and having to rely increasingly on

borrowed money. The amount required and the length of time the finance is required for will have a bearing on the sources of finance to be approached. Lenders will want to see budgets.
6 Adjusting its internal management structure to cope with growth.

7.2 Uncertainty in Budgeting

Teams of full-time economists are unable to forecast economic growth rates but the fact that forecasts cannot be made with certainty does not mean that forecasts should not be attempted.

The danger is that when uncertainty is high – and few people can recall times in their business lives when they were operating in times of great certainty – there is a temptation to avoid planning. 'With the threat of a nuclear war why should I bother planning? This is exactly the reaction of a rabbit caught in the headlights and is a policy that is not to be recommended.

Strangely, although many people will venture strong opinions on future levels of inflation or interest rates and world economic growth, when they tackle their own budgeting they tend to assume that 'things will go on as they are'. When inflation rates are 15% they build 15% inflation into their budgets for the following year. It is essential to recognize that probably the least likely outcome is that 'things will go on as they are'. Budgeting should take account of a range of possible changes in markets and costs. Budgets must be adjustable and sensitive to unexpected changes. Figure 7.1 illustrates the danger of the 'same as before' approach which produces inflexible budgets.

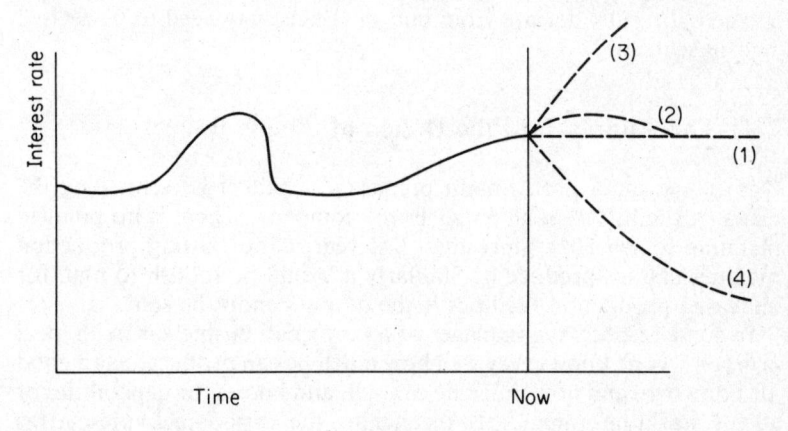

Figure 7.1

Managing Your Company's Finances

Which is the likeliest direction interest rates will take from now? It is suggested that the *least* likely is (1) in Figure 7.1. We may not know which outcome is the *most* likely but budgets can be prepared to take some account of the range of possibilities.

7.3 Basic Budgetary Control

Budgeting and budgetary control is not simply forecasting what will happen. Certainly business forecasting is important. The small businessman should be able to have some feel for the future demand for his product, the likely effect of changes in competition, inflation rates and so on. What he can do is decide on his objectives for some time ahead, work out what he will need to achieve them and finally compare carefully what he actually achieves with what he thought would happen. The reasons for variances from the budget levels set should indicate areas for management action.

Specifically the chief executive needs to:

1. Set his overall objectives for the business. Only he knows where he wants the business to go. He may desire profit, sales, market share, 'going public', having the most comprehensive range of products in the market or have some esoteric motive for running the business. It is necessary to state what the objective is.
2. Create a management or organizational structure in which lines of authority, responsibility and accountability are clearly laid down.
3. Prepare plans for a specific period and budgets which, if met, will realize the plans.
4. Monitor the results regularly and take management action when actual results deviate from budget. Plans may need to be revised subsequently.

7.4 The Approach to the Design of Simple Budgets

One of the main problems in preparing a budget is reconciling the views of the different activities in the company. There is no point in planning to sell 50% more than last year if the existing production facilities cannot produce it. Similarly it would be foolish to plan for increased production facilities if the output cannot be sold.

In some respects the manager of a very small business is in an ideal position. As he knows very well how much he can produce, has a good idea of where and how much he can sell, and knows the capabilities of all his staff, he is regularly reconciling the various activities in his mind and planning can often come easily. What he needs is the

Budgetary Control

discipline of writing down his budget and comparing it regularly with results. For the more developed small or medium-sized business the MD cannot be an expert in every field and must rely on his managers' views. Indeed it is vitally important that he takes his managers' views on, for example, sales potential into account; much damage can be done by imposing unachievable targets and budgets on subordinate staff.

The budgeting and control process should proceed along these lines.

7.4.1 *Budgeting Sales, Production and Cost Levels*

An estimate is made for each activity of what it could achieve in the coming period (of say one year) and of what it will require to do so. The sales budget may start with the goal of achieving a 1% market share and this will be translated into £500,000 of sales or 1,000 units; to achieve this, two more salesmen and some £5,000 of advertising backup will be needed.

The production budget may be stated initially at 1,500 units (£750,000 sales value) and would require a new machine costing £30,000.

7.4.2 *Reconciliation*

The two forecasts must be reconciled and decisions made, on the basis of profitability and practical achievement, on whether the capital expenditure would yield more profit even if it means adding skill more salesmen to the team or whether the market cannot absorb the additional 500 units. The effect on the budgets of the sales or production forecasts not being met must be assessed; the budgets must be flexible enough to allow for unexpected changes during the budgeting period.

Capital expenditure, additional costs and income, higher stocks, debtors and creditors all affect the cash requirement. This is usually the final determinant in the reconciliation – how much finance is available. In later chapters the sources of finance and the presentation of a case is looked at in detail. Finance is more generally available and exists in more varied forms than many small companies realize; while, therefore, all budgets must finally be reconciled to the finance available to support them, those preparing budgets should not feel overly constrained. A well-prepared budget and cash forecast can often ensure that financial support will be forthcoming.

7.4.3 *Control Systems*

The value of a budgeting system lies in the facility afforded for monitoring progress and identifying variances. The responsibility for each budget must be clearly defined to avoid recrimination.

The setting of budgets in each activity and their reconciliation are considered in Chapters 8, 9 and 10.

7.4.4 Time Scale

In 7.3 above it was stated that a chief executive should state his objectives. This global, overall or 'corporate' planning must take place before budgeting can begin. If a motorist sets off to drive he usually has some specific destination in mind and some idea of how he will get there. Without some basic plan the journey may be interesting – even very exciting – but potentially frustrating, inefficient and, in financial terms, highly dangerous. Worse, if he does not know where he is going, how will he know if he has arrived, or how rapid his progress is, or what corrective action he should take?

In corporate planning a basic goal is set but it must be set in the knowledge that it is achievable within the time-scale of the plan. A goal to be a larger corporation than ICI in ten years would be impossible. However if the businessman lists the strengths of his business – geographical location, advanced custom-built products, supply of skilled labour, speed of response – and its weaknesses, an achievable goal can be set. Its achievement may depend on major and wide ranging changes.

Budgets should be for a sensible period. One week or one month is too short. Equally five year forecasts are notoriously difficult to make yet some changes can take as long as five years to have full effect. One year is usually taken although this may not be the financial year of the company.

There can be times of the year when it is easier to forecast sales than others – particularly in agriculture or following major industrial exhibitions.

The monitoring systems must show results during, not at the end of, the budget period. No businessman can afford to wait for the visit of the auditors to find out if he made a profit in the most recent trading year. More importantly, as the budgeting control system is a tool of management, regular monthly or quarterly assessments of progress are essential so that corrective action can be taken.

7.5 Action Points

1. Plan, however uncertain the future is.
2. Decide overall objectives.
3. Plan and monitor results, comparing actual with budget.
4. Take corrective action.

VIII
Capital Expenditure Budget

8.1 Introduction

This chapter considers budgeting for capital expenditure and concentrates on the justifying of such expenditure in financial terms. Although some sophisticated techniques are referred to, none is dealt with in detail; the aim of the chapter is to develop the correct approach to budgeting for capital spending.

8.2 What is Meant by Capital Expenditure

The accounting definition of capital expenditure is expenditure on assets which are not for resale in the ordinary course of business but are to be held for the purposes of earning revenue. Thus buildings, plant, equipment, furniture and motor cars are all easily identifiable as capital items. In Chapter 2 the main components of a balance sheet were considered and examples of fixed assets were taken as property, plant and motor vehicles. However major advertising programmes, sales promotions, or research and development projects, can also be considered to be capital expenditure. If a major research programme is undertaken it may seem unreasonable to reduce the profit in any year by the cost of the research because there may be great benefits to come in the future. Some businesses treat the research cost as a fixed asset, reducing its value by depreciation in charges as the benefits (e.g. from sales of a new product) begin to flow in. The cost of the asset is therefore spread over the period of its useful (earning) life.

There are dangers in this. The expenditure on research may yield no benefit, the major advertising programme may not increase sales. The accounting bodies now recommend that, except in special circumstances, such expenditures are treated as costs incurred in a given year which reduce profit. Any benefit following in future years is a bonus. This practice has the merit of conservatism. Moreover it takes some account of the movement of cash. The money on research is being spent today, not spread over the next few years. No matter how great the sales increase the money is less valuable in three years' time than it is now – not just because of inflation but because the money could be at least earning interest over the three years if it was available now.

8.3 Justifying Capital Spending

All major capital expenditures should have to be justified in their claims on the firm's resource of cash. It is difficult to be dogmatic about the size of expenditure which qualifies. One firm in the South of England with a turnover of £10 million has all capital items over £10 approved individually by the full board. This may appear inefficient but capital spending is an area where money can be tied up with no immediately apparent prospect of any return. In a very small business, small capital expenditure can be monitored fairly easily; as the business expands much authority for day-to-day transactions, such as inventory build-up, can be delegated because these transactions do not usually tie up capital for long periods and the justification for such expenditure is often the dictates of the market. Capital spending has no such natural disciplines. The purchase of even humble items such as a typist's chair or desk needs justification. The rest of this chapter deals with the justification of major capital expenditure.

The process of justifying the expenditure is the kernel of capital budgeting.

All businesses have a finite supply of money though an almost infinite number of opportunities for investing it. Put simply, the purchase of a new machine can only be justified if it earns a return greater than any other conceivable use to which the money can be put. Where a number of projects can be financed these can be ranked in order of priority on the basis of expected returns.

A company may have surplus cash which it can invest in a new machine or put on deposit in the money market; the predicted earnings from the machine would have to exceed the expected interest on the deposit to make the expenditure worthwhile.

Often a business will have to borrow money to finance the machinery purchase; the machine must earn at least the interest cost of the borrowing to justify the expenditure. Just how the returns over a period can be measured and compared with cost of capital will be considered later in this chapter.

Capital Expenditure Budget

8.4 Measuring Returns

Small capital items, those where financial quantification is difficult but which can be justified on other grounds (e.g. a lunch room for employees) and those which are clearly very highly profitable should be excluded from any calculation of returns. Returns should be measured only where future income and costs can be reasonably estimated and where there is some doubt about the advisability of the investment or there are competing claims for the available capital. It is really, therefore, marginal decisions which are best suited to techniques for measuring returns.

8.5 Methods of Investment Appraisal

There are many textbooks which cover the complexities of deciding whether or not a particular investment in, say, machinery is worthwhile. There are four basic methods which are used by small and medium-sized businesses. Two of those take account of the timing of the expenditure and the income which arises from the asset over its useful life. The first two which are considered below do not.

8.5.1 *Accounting Rate of Return*

Accounting rate of return or average rate of return calculations vary. They all attempt to relate the accounting profits expected to result from a project to the balance sheet value of that project. The formula is often:

$$\frac{\text{Average accounting profit}}{\text{Average balance sheet value}}$$

If the accounting rate of return is greater than the cost of capital – say, simply, the cost of borrowing money to finance the project – then it is worthwhile going ahead with the purchase. If the accounting return from the project is less than the cost of financing it, then clearly the project should not be undertaken.

Example

A company can buy a machine for £40,000. It will make profits of £5,000, £10,000, £15,000 and £20,000 in the four years of its life. It is assumed that profit is the same as cash flow less depreciation charge; that is, all sales are cash sales, all purchases are paid for immediately and no stocks are held. The machine will be worth nothing at the end of the four years.

The cash flows are:

Now (purchase of machine) − £40,000 (cash paid out)
Year 1   + £ 5,000 (cash received)
2   + £10,000
3   + £15,000
4   + £20,000

If the cost of borrowing money is 10% and depreciation is 25% in each of the four years the accounting rate of return is as shown in table 8.1.

Table 8.1 Profit & Loss Accounts

	Accounting Cash Inflow	Depreciation		Profit/Loss
Year 1	5,000	10,000	Loss	5,000
2	10,000	10,000		−
3	15,000	10,000	Profit	5,000
4	20,000	10,000	Profit	10,000
				10,000

Average account profit − 4   £ 2,500

Balance Sheet

	Asset value at beginning of year	End of year	Average Value
Year 1	40,000	30,000	35,000
2	30,000	20,000	25,000
3	20,000	10,000	15,000
4	10,000	−	5,000
			80,000

Average balance sheet value − 4   £20,000

$$\text{Accounting Rate of Return} = \frac{2,500}{20,000} = 12.5\%$$

The investment in this project would be considered worthwhile because the return is higher than the 10% cost of borrowing.

The major drawback of this method is that it ignores the timing of expenditure and income. In this case expenditure is substantial in the early years, income substantial in later years. The effect of this timing

Capital Expenditure Budget

difference would be to make the project not worthwhile as will be seen later with what are called Discounted Cash Flow techniques.

The Accounting Rate of Return method is not recommended for investment appraisal.

8.5.2 *Payback*

This method is simpler in that it does not involve calculations of average balance sheet values and accounting profits. The 'payback period' is the time that will elapse between spending money on a project and recovering that initial expenditure from income generated by the project. This method is used by many small businesses. A machine, it is said, 'will pay for itself in three years'. The idea is simple and appealing, but in practice there can be difficulties.

Example

A company has £40,000 available. It can invest in one of three machines. The cash flows (net income actually received in cash) over four years are as shown in Table 8.2.

Table 8.2

	Machine A £	Machine B £	Machine C £
Cash paid for machine now:	(40,000)	(40,000)	(40,000)
Year 1	15,000	15,000	20,000
2	10,000	10,000	20,000
3	25,000	25,000	10,000
4	–	15,000	15,000
Payback Period	3 years	3 years	3 years

All three machines recover their initial investment by the end of the third year of operation. Machine B has an identical cash flow to Machine A but continues producing income in year 4 – an extra £15,000 – and must be preferred to Machine A. Machine B and Machine C produce an identical amount of income but Machine C produces the cash return earlier than Machine B. It is desirable to have cash sooner rather than later. Machine C is the preferred investment.

The illustrations above demonstrate the shortcomings of the payback method. Timing of expenditure and income are not allowed for and because of this the method should not normally be used for investment appraisal. However, where early cash returns are important (e.g. where a company is highly geared) payback can be the only practical test.

8.5.3 Net Present Value

This technique takes into account the timing of payment and receipts of cash during the life of a project and is therefore superior to Payback and Accounting Rate of Return as a method of investment appraisal.

To understand the Net Present Value method it is necessary to understand Discounted Cash Flow. The words Discounted Cash Flow or the initials DCF strike fear into some people; the words have an air of mystery. In fact the idea of discounting cash flows is quite simple and has been hinted at earlier in this chapter.

8.6 Discounted Cash Flow

Basically it is better to have £100 now rather than in one year's time. This is not because of inflation as such but because £100 could be invested to produce interest, dividend or a cash return of some kind during the year. How much more £100 is worth *now* compared with one year from now depends on what return could be obtained from investing it. If £100 can be invested at 10% per annum then the value today (the present value) of £100 in one year's time is £91.

That is if £91 was invested today for one year it would attract £9 of interest bringing the capital sum up to £100. So £100 in one year's time, 'discounted' at 10% is worth £91 today. The 10% is called the discount rate.

The higher the discount rate the less valuable will be the returns in later years. The choice of the correct discount rate is therefore important. For most small businesses the discount rate will be the cost of capital – the cost of borrowing additional funds to finance the project. If money is borrowed at 12% per annum then any returning cash will be used to repay the borrowing and 'earn' 12% return. All cash flows should be discounted at that rate.

Some larger companies take a more sophisticated approach and have a required rate of return on all investments. This is usually higher than the cost of borrowed capital and reflects their cost of shareholders' funds as well. So they are not only comparing the relative profitability of Machine A and Machine B; they are also

Capital Expenditure Budget

specifying that the machines must be sufficiently profitable. One machine could be earning a return of 15%, the other 16%, but the required rate for all projects may be 17% and so neither machine would be purchased. This is an over-simplification of the process but it demonstrates that the individual capital budgeting decision cannot be made without regard to overall corporate objectives.

8.7 Net present Value

If a project investment is being considered the owners of a business are seeking to improve the value of the business in today's terms (the present value). All the income less all the costs of a project could be discounted over the years of its life to a present value; if the value was greater than zero the project would be worthwhile. Assume that £80 is spent on a machine, £100 will be earned one year from now and the machine then scrapped. Money costs 10% per annum. £100 discounted at 10% has a present value of £91. After deducting the £80 cost there is an £11 increase in the net present value of the business. If, however, the £100 was earned at the end of the second year its present value would only be £83 and the decision is only just a marginal one.

There is a formula for calculating what a sum of money in the future is worth today at a given discount rate. It is simpler to state using an example.

8.8 Example of Discounted Cash Flow

A company will receive £10,000 per annum for four years. Money costs 10% per annum. The present value of the four cash flows of £10,000 is as shown in Table 8.3.

Table 8.3

$$\text{PV (Present Value)} = \frac{10{,}000}{(1 + 10\%)^n} + \frac{10{,}000}{(1 + 10\%)^n} + \frac{10{,}000}{(1 + 10\%)^n} + \frac{10{,}000}{(1 + 10\%)^n}$$

Note

The formula is

$$\frac{£}{(1 + i)^n} = 9{,}100 + 8{,}300 + 7{,}500 + 6{,}800 = £31{,}700$$

where 'i' is the interest or discount rate and 'n' is the number of years from the start of the project.

Managing Your Company's Finances

In Table 8.3 an outlay now of less than £31,700 to produce £10,000 per annum for four years is a worthwhile investment. The net present value is greater than nothing; there is thus an increase in the value of the business in terms of present value.

In practice, Discounted Cash Flow tables are available and calculators can do the arithmetic.

8.9 Example of Net Present Value

In Table 8.2 above the payback periods and the cash returns of Machine B and Machine C were the same but there was a feeling that Machine C was a better buy because the cash flows were received earlier. This can now be proved using Net Present Value techniques as in Table 8.4.

Table 8.4

	Machine B		Machine B Discounted at 10%		Machine C		Machine C Discounted at 10%
Purchase −	40,000	−	40,000	−	40,000	−	40,000
Years 1 +	5,000	+	4,100	+	10,000	+	9,100
2 +	10,000	+	8,300	+	20,000	+	16,700
3 +	25,000	+	18,800	+	10,000	+	7,500
4 +	25,000	+	10,200	+	15,000	+	10,200
Net income +	£25,000	NPV	1,100	+	15,000	NPV	3,500

Although Machine B's total income is greater Machine C's cash inflows are more valuable because they are received earlier. Note that both machines produce a positive net present value. Both are worthwhile investments.

Net Present Value (NPV) is recommended as a valuable method of appraising investment.

8.10 Internal Rate of Return

This is the other major Discounted Cash Flow method for appraising investments. To calculate Net Present Value in Table 8.4 a discount rate was used. The Internal Rate of Return is the rate at which discounted cash flows give a Net Present Value of zero.

Capital Expenditure Budget

Example

Taking the example of Machine C above, a discount rate of 10% shows a positive Net Present Value. A higher discount rate will reduce the NPV. The only way to arrive at the internal rate of return is by trial and error. Calculators or computers, if available, can take care of much of this arithmetic. A discount rate of 14% gives:

$$\text{NPV} = -£40{,}000 + \frac{10{,}000}{(1.14)} + \frac{20{,}000}{(1.14)^2} + \frac{10{,}000}{(1.14)^3} + \frac{15{,}000}{(1.14)^4}$$

$$= -£40{,}000 + 8{,}800 + 15{,}400 + 6{,}700 + 8{,}900$$

$$= -£200$$

The discount rate of 14% gives a very small negative NPV. A discount rate of just under 14% is the Internal Rate of Return (IRR).

Using this method the company would consider whether this return is high enough. Many companies have a rate of return below which no object is worthwhile.

The drawback of this method is that when comparing a large and small project it can give misleading results. A small project may have a much higher IRR than a large one but the large one is actually yielding more profit and will have a higher Net Present Value. Although this method is widely used among larger companies its drawbacks must be borne in mind.

8.11 Calculations

This chapter has attempted to communicate the dangers of assessing investment decisions without a consideration of the timing of cash outflows and inflows. The NPV method is recommended for larger projects. Tables for discount rates are available in any textbook on the subject. Small businessmen may feel that the last two methods are too sophisticated. A detailed mathematical background is not needed despite the apparent sophistication. Even if the calculation is left to others, those responsible for investment decisions should have a feel for the effect timing has on present values of future earnings. Because of this effect the sensitivity of cash forecasts to changes in the market, delays in production, delivery and payment by customers must be examined carefully. If there is a risk of delay in receiving cash, the effect should be calculated.

8.12 Action Points

1 Justify capital expenditure.

Managing Your Company's Finances

2 Measure the returns expected from expenditure.
3 Take the timing of cash flows into account.

8.13 Forms

Specimen forms attached are for the Capital Expenditure Budget and the Capital Budget Report which covers the progress of major capital expenditure items.

The format for cash forecasting which is necessary before calculating any discounted return is explained in Chapter 4.

Capital Expenditure Budget

Capital   **Expenditure**   **Budget**
£000's

Item No.	Accountable Manager	Description of Capital Item	Start Date	Finish Date	Cost		Total
					This Budget	After Budget	
Carried forward end of this period							
				Total			
Start budget period							
				Total			
					Total		

Capital Budget Report

Period..................

Name of Manager accountable	Description of Capital Item	Expected completion date		Budgeted cost		Actual expenditure to date		Actual estimated further expenditure			Estimated actual cost	Cost variances
		Original	Revised	Original	Revised	This year	Total	This year	After this year	Total		
Completed previously												
Completed this period												
	Total completed £											
In progress												
	Total in progress £											
Not yet started												
	Total not yet started £											
	Total £											

IX
Sales and Production Forecasts

9.1 Introduction

It is not possible to calculate the returns from an investment, and therefore decide whether or not to go ahead, without first estimating the level of sales and the capacity for and costs of producing the goods to be sold. This chapter deals with sales and production forecasting.

9.2 Sales Forecasting

9.2.1 The Market

Any small business must know which market it operates in and understand the reason for any sales it makes in the market. Is it because the product or service is inherently better than those of competitors? It is cheaper, delivered more quickly, given a better after-sales service?

Small firms sometimes pay for a market survey undertaken by consultants. While such surveys tell us that the market for, say, a left-handed widget in the Western Hemisphere is £123 million per annum, this knowledge may be of little use if we are aiming to sell £123,000 worth of goods next year after last year's sales of £100,000. Our market share is tiny (0.1%); our efforts are unlikely to offend market leaders. However what we do not know is the name and location of the buyers of our next year's output.

For most small companies the estimate of sales volume is a very practical exercise. It should consist of finding out the requirements of customers and the future requirements of end-users, and considering these in the context of the trends of the market.

Managing Your Company's Finances

9.2.2 Existing Customers

The sales force or those in direct contact with customers should be able to elicit a rough idea of requirements for the following year (or budget period). If a customer's business is expanding, opportunities should exist for increasing supplies to his business. Contacts at different levels with customers can help to build up a picture of their future requirements. Often a deliveryman or storeman can provide early warning of plans for expansion which could mean an opportunity to sell. A useful exercise is to list all regular customers and put down against the names an estimate of their requirements over the following year. These estimates are then assigned to a probability rating; if there is only a 10% chance that a particular customer will place an order for £100,000 this is unlikely to mean that he will place an order for £10,000. However if the probability is applied over a whole range of customers a reasonably accurate estimate can be assembled. Each first guess is reduced to 10%, 50% or whatever the probability is of getting the business. The resultant smaller estimates, none of which are likely orders individually, will give an overall estimate which is likely to be achieved. The discipline of going through a customer list will concentrate effort on the most likely sources of business.

9.2.3 New Customers/Markets

Other users in the existing market can be identified and an estimate made of the likely level of sales.

What potential users exist in other markets – that is users outside the geographical area now serviced or users in other fields of activity who at present are now known to be users of the product? The first area could mean moving into export markets or simply recruiting a salesman to cover, say the South West of England. The second route could mean a long term strategy, convincing a whole industry of non-users to think about your product.

Either way additional costs will be incurred and the sales outcome is less certain than with new users in existing markets – and far less certain than the requirements of existing customers. It is important that sales forecasts are conservative enough to reflect this uncertainty and that additional costs are budgeted for.

9.2.4 New Products/Obsolescence

Any product or service has a life cycle. In its early days acceptance may be low but it reaches a peak; the trick is to recognize that demand is about to peak when there is still time to redevelop the product, alter the service provided, design a new product or move into a new business altogether.

Where a product is fairly technical, obsolescence is perhaps a greater threat – e.g. in electronics. However at least obsolescence is recognized in that industry as an ever-present problem which has to be overcome. Prices can be adjusted to reflect the research and development costs which must be recouped. In apparently more stable industries less attention is paid to obsolescence and yet it can mean both a threat and an opportunity for small firms which by their nature are much quicker to react to changing circumstances.

9.2.5 Market Trends

The obsolescence in 9.2.4 above can arise as a result of genuine research and development as in the growth of the plastics industry and the replacement of many natural materials with man-made fibres. The rise in some world commodity prices may be removing the price-competitiveness of some plastics and synthetic materials and reversing the substitution process. Economic recession and inflation should mean bad news for everyone but opportunities are often created. Convenience catering was at first expensive and status oriented, but an example of a market opportunity was freezer foods, where, later, real savings could be demonstrated.

All small businessmen must look at the changes in market conditions. They cannot be expected to forecast them accurately – even US Presidents cannot do that – but they must use their hunches in providing a context for longer term planning. Since economic factors cannot be controlled, allowance must be made for them in estimating sales volume.

9.2.6 Pricing

So far only the volume of sales has been considered. The unit selling price determines how much money actually comes in from sales and can affect the volume of sales by making the product more or less competitive on price.

The price at which a product sells usually is and ought to be determined by what the market will bear.

Some theorists would argue that the selling price is manufacturing cost plus overheads plus a margin for profit. Certainly if selling price does not give a margin for profit the cost structure, efficiency of production, the range of products and their suitability for the market need to be looked at fundamentally. The ultimate profit margin however will depend on supply and demand.

The structure of and budgeting for costs is covered in Chapter 10. For the purposes of sales forecasting and pricing in particular it is necessary to recognize that in all companies some costs are fixed and others vary with the level of activity. If a factory is running at 50% capacity its products are saddled with a very high manufacturing cost per unit. If production increases to 100% capacity then manufacturing costs per unit are halved but any business basing its selling price directly on either cost per unit is asking for trouble. In the first case it could well be priced out of the market; in the second it may well be incurring losses and would not be earning the return it deserves for efficient manufacturing.

It is well known that few costs vary directly with levels of activity in the small company. Instead there is a 'step function', that is, one minute all ten employees are working flat out, the next two extra employees are taken on, increasing the wages cost by 20% while activity levels take longer to come into line. Even worse is the factory extension which may take months before it begins to contribute to throughput and then not at 100% capacity. One minute unit production costs are very low, the next rather high.

For small companies in an orderly market, the market leader usually sets the price at which an efficient producer can sell. The market leader has all the advantages of size – bigger plants, longer production runs, better distribution. The small businessman can do all the theoretical pricing calculations he wants (and there are books available dealing with pricing alone) but in practice he has to price according to competition – higher prices but better delivery, product or service; lower prices which he hopes will give him the volume of sales to compensate for lower margins. He may have to give a little on price and provide a better service because he lacks the credibility of the market leader. If, however, he is only selling because of his price differential, his is a vulnerable position.

Pricing is looked at in more detail in Chapter 12.

9.3 Production Forecasting

Production forecasting is something of a Cinderella in business forecasting. External advice is often heavily financially biased; the small businessman will be expected to produce cash flows, profit statements and forecast balance sheets. The businessman himself is usually more at home with his market than anywhere else; his forecasting is therefore likely to be very sales-biased. What are often forgotten are production capacity, costs and efficiencies; too little strategic thinking is done about production and sometimes there is too much concentration on only one aspect of it.

Sales and Production Forecasts

An example was the small Scottish manufacturer of wooden trays for fruit packing in the Glasgow fruit market. The manufacturing process was simple; a few men with staple guns or stapling machines put together about ten or twelve slats of wood. Much effort was expended on considering the introduction of new stapling machines to increase productivity and therefore profit. In reality the company was a timber importer which added little value to the raw material. If timber was bought well profits resulted, if there were buying errors losses resulted. The sensitive area of production was the trading end and manufacture could have been 50% or 100% efficient with little effect on profit.

This illustrates a lack of strategic thought in the area of production. Sometimes, however, production is forgotten almost entirely. In the early 1970s a small company was started to manufacture an electronic product. The management team had impressive backgrounds in large companies. They researched the market thoroughly, forecast sales, landed important long term orders, organized factory space, hired staff, prepared cash flows based on their sales forecasts and successfully approached their bank for finance. The first four pre-production units were made satisfactorily. Unfortunately when full production began no-one seemed quite sure whether it was on a batch or flow line basis, certain components ran out because stock levels were inadequate causing delays in delivery, supervision was inadequate and quality suffered. Goods were returned by customers for repair causing greater strain on productive capacity and the cash flow suffered alarmingly. Not only did the hiccup in sales affect profits, the unwillingness of customers to pay for the faulty goods meant that there was virtually no cash flowing in for two or three months. The company had little fat and finally was forced into liquidation by creditors. At the time other factors were adversely affecting the company's performance but the seeds of its ultimate failure were sown in the poor planning and forecasting of production.

It is hoped that the foregoing examples will help to put in context the following remarks on production forecasting. Production in a manufacturing business consists of obtaining and storing of raw materials, the application of labour and machinery to these materials and the control of levels of work in progress and finished goods.

Production can of course be relatively simple to forecast as with the selling of machine time, working on other people's materials on free issue or indeed the selling of the time of highly skilled people. The charge out rate per hour of the man or machine, the level of chargeable time needed to break even and in most cases the number of useful hours which can be worked in any given period can be calculated fairly accurately. Where, for example, a team of technical people in a laboratory is estimating the number of chargeable hours needed to solve a problem, a substantial margin must be built in to allow for over-run.

This over-run problem applies also to manufacturing industries where special products are being made. The previous experience of long production runs is of little help.

9.3.1 Raw Materials and Components

For smooth production, materials and parts must be available at the right time in the right place. It is necessary to know:

(a) How soon materials will arrive, ready to use, allowing the placing of a purchase order.
(b) What is the usage rate of each type of raw material.
(c) How large a buffer stock of materials is needed.

The key here is flexibility. The material must be to hand but there is no point in going to extreme lengths to achieve this. A number of timber importers created great problems for themselves in 1974/75 by trying to guarantee a supply of timber. The market was buoyant, inflationary 'stock profits' were easy to make and some importers arranged supplies eighteen months ahead on a firm basis. When the market collapsed timber continued to pour in from Scandinavia and Russia and the resulting over-stocking problem destroyed company liquidity.

A minimum working stock, re-order level and order quantity can be determined relative to production schedules. The minimum stock ought to be related to planned sales. The material content of sales for the period as adjusted for opening and closing stocks will give the amount of material to be ordered during the period. Firms in a seasonal or fashion business will have extreme stocking requirements at different times and probably an irregular production schedule. Few businesses have totally continuous schedules and some (e.g. in the cider industry) spend some weeks in every year in overhauling equipment and a few months in peak overtime production.

For the small and medium-sized company, any benefit to be gained by ordering large quantities of materials is offset by the loss of flexibility occasioned by tying up capital. Some would argue that there is money to be made by over-ordering or holding large stocks in an inflationary environment; it is more likely that the secret is to have an up-to-date pricing policy and to keep at a minimum level the capital tied up in current assets.

9.3.2 Labour

Levels of achieved production related to useful hours available gives a measure of productive capacity of labour. Although labour is clearly a cost which varies with the level of activity, no small firm should be deluded into thinking that the relationship is exactly direct. To increase capacity a new man is taken on; he will not be able to reach established standards of output for some days or perhaps weeks and this assumes that labour of the right quality is available. Further, if total capacity is not needed according to the sales forecast it may not be correct policy to lay off workers. The small businessman must ask if he is in a long-term business; if he is he will have to recognize that he cannot lay off and expect to be able to rehire with ease particularly skilled men. There are likely, then, to be unavoidable inefficiencies which creep in and alter the calculation of available labour capacity. Perhaps the most important of these is time spent in supervising. The example of the electronics company showed what can happen when no-one is supervising effectively the production process, including stock control. An estimate of productive labour capacity must allow for supervision, training, holidays, sickness and down time.

9.3.3 Plant

The output of a manufacturing plant per hour is relatively easily calculated, but, as with labour, a new machine may take time to bed down (a man's learning curve) will require servicing (training), will break down (become ill) occasionally and will become obsolete. Moreover in any kind of production flow it is important that new machinery does not process material more slowly or quickly than the rest of the production line – otherwise bottlenecks develop. The costs of operating a plant are considered in Chapter 10.

9.4 Action Points

1 Ask what market you are in, what product or service you are selling and who your customers really are.
2 Forecast sales practically by considering the requirements of existing customers, new customers/markets and possible demand for new products.
3 Think about the areas of production to which profits are sensitive.
4 Plan the movement of materials carefully.

9.5 Forms

Specimen budgeting forms which cover the areas of sales and production as well as overhead costs are shown at the end of Chapter 10.

X
Cost Budgets

10.1 Introduction

In this chapter the problems arising from budgeting costs, both direct and indirect, are considered. The individual cost headings should coincide as far as possible with those in the detailed profit and loss account (prepared for internal use) of the business to facilitate comparison but more detailed analysis may be required. Profit and loss accounts are usually set out in a logical style with direct costs being deducted from sales revenue first, then indirect operating expenses and finally financial costs such as overdraft interest.

10.2 Profit and Loss

A typical manufacturing company's trading and profit and loss account could be set out as in Table 10.1.

10.3 Monitoring Cost Budgets

The purpose of cost budgets is the control of costs. Regular, usually monthly, comparison of actual with budgeted costs allows for early management action where necessary.

Some expenses do not occur evenly over the year; care must be taken to increase particular monthly budgets to cater for items which do not recur every month such as quarterly rentals.

A simple examination of the reasons for significant deviations (or 'variances') from the budget is instructive but may not be enough. The flexibility mentioned in 10.5 below works both ways; a sales department that is spending in line with its cost budget but failing to get sales may need more urgent action than an apparently prodigal sales manager who regularly beats his sales target.

Table 10.1 Profit & Loss Account – Year 2

BUDGET (YEAR 2)		COMPARATIVE YEAR 1
Sales		£500,000
Less: Direct Costs:		
Materials (after adjusting for opening and closing stocks)	200,000	
Wages	150,000	350,000
Gross Profit (30%)		150,000
Less: Indirect Costs – Production		
Rent & Rates		
Heat, Light, Power		
Wages – indirect (e.g. supervising)	50,000	
Repairs and Renewals		
Depreciation – machines		
Packing		
Indirect – Selling Expenses		
Salaries & Sales Commission		
Travelling & Entertaining	20,000	
Advertising		
Indirect – Administration Expenses		
Salaries (e.g. book-keeper)		
Postage, telephone	20,000	
Indirect – Other		
Directors' Salaries		
Audit fee, loan interest, pensions	20,000	110,000
Net Profit Before Tax		£ 40,000

The manufacturing company whose profit and loss account is shown earlier in Table 10.1 has a gross profit percentage of 30%. The reason for any change in this arises from sales or cost variances. In the case of an increase this could result from an adverse cost variance (an overspend) with a correspondingly greater increase in sales revenue. The effect on profit is more important than the fact that there has been an overspend in one budget heading. Moreover an increase in gross margin may have been achieved by raising prices but promising a better after sales service so that increased indirect costs will swallow up most or all of the benefit.

Without over complicating the budgeting process in a small business it can be useful to look at the effect on profits of varying levels of sales

Managing Your Company's Finances

and a given mix of fixed and variable costs (see break even chart below).

Many expenses are genuinely fixed in that they either do not change at all for some years (e.g. rent) or partly fixed in that they have to be met regardless of the level of business activity. Direct costs vary directly with the level of activity in theory; in practice the cost of labour does not fall directly with a fall in production or sales.

10.4 Break-Even Chart

A simple but useful management tool is the break-even chart (Figure 10.1). If the Profit and Loss Account in Table 10.1 above is taken as a basis, it may be decided that all administration and 'other' indirect costs are fixed, that three-quarters of the selling costs do not vary with levels of activity and that 70% of production overheads are also fixed for the budget year. This gives total fixed costs of £100,000. The effect on the company's profits of different levels of sales may be calculated.

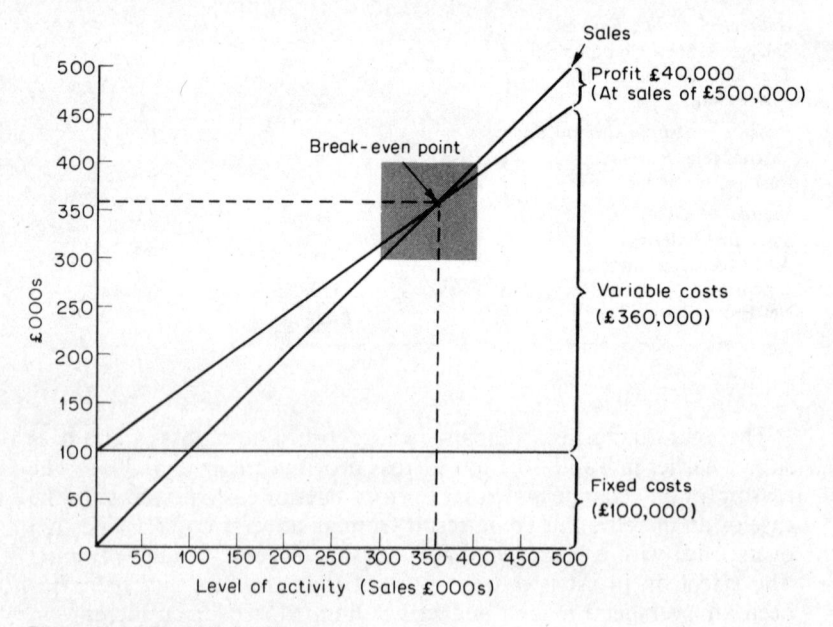

Figure 10.1 Break-Even Chart

The horizontal axis shows the sales volume, the vertical axis shows value in £s, whether costs, income or profit. The fixed costs of the business are £100,000 whatever the level of activity. The volume of

Cost Budgets

activity is best measured in terms of turnover value. If the forecast sales of £500,000 are met a net profit of about £40,000 will result. If sales fall below £360,000 a loss will be sustained. Clearly the more level the lines on the graph the lower will be the sensitivity of profit to changes in the level of sales. This is because the fixed element of costs are higher. Where the lines are steeper, small changes in the levels of activity can mean substantial changes in profits.

The break-even chart is a crude tool. It assumes that the behaviour of income and costs will be constant whatever the level of activity (e.g. no changes in sales price to increase volume), a simplistic division of costs into convenient categories of fixed and variable, no change in productivity and a constant sales mix. Nevertheless for each business it highlights graphically the sensitivity of profit to changes in volume.

10.5 Responsibility, Accountability and Flexibility

Just as the sales manager is responsible for the sales budget so each departmental manager must be responsible and accountable for the costs of his department. In a very small business the owner may control every function and can therefore set the budgets. In most businesses, however, there is sufficient delegation of authority to ensure that a manager must believe his cost budgets are reasonable and workable. Cost budgets must never be imposed on a manager without a dialogue between him and his supervisor; no manager can be held to account for an overspend on a cost budget he always maintained was too low.

Managers should also only be accountable for those costs over which they have control; if the production manager of the manufacturing company in 10.3 above has no say in depreciation policy, there is no point in including it in his departmental budget. The budgets must also be flexible. A sales manager may, in beating his sales target, exceed his telephone cost budget by month 9 but no-one would suggest seriously that he and his team stop making phone calls altogether for the last three months of the year. A contingency amount should be set aside so that justifiable overspending can occur within the limits of overall budgeted costs.

10.6 Direct Costs

10.6.1 Materials

Where complex products or special pieces of equipment are manufactured, a parts list is likely to exist with estimated costs to facilitate pricing. In such cases estimating material costs for a given volume of production is relatively straightforward. Where production is simple or non-existent (e.g. in a trading company) the material cost of sales can be estimated from past experience. Material wastage must be allowed for. In all cases inflationary increases in the cost of materials must be taken into account. In the very high inflationary conditions of 1974/76 when wage increases exceeded 30% and the Retail Price Index annual increase reached 26% many small firms did not pass on increased costs. Market conditions often dictated this but the costing/budgeting/pricing systems were often incapable of reacting quickly enough. Profits seemed very high but proved to be illusory. Stocks of raw materials had to be replaced at inflated prices.

10.6.2 Labour

Without established standards for the number of hours of direct and supervisory or ancillary labour required for given volumes of production it is difficult to produce labour budgets.

Most accountants would argue that budgets for labour costs cannot be set without establishing the number of man hours of direct, supervisory and ancillary labour required for each job (in the case of 'one-off' or 'specials' manufacture), process or unit of production. Variances from standard budgets could be due to overtime working or some production inefficiencies; tying them down to specific products or stages of production can facilitate management action. The cost and inconvenience of timing operations and setting standards may, however, offset the benefits to be gained from being able to pinpoint the reason for higher labour costs as a percentage of sales volume.

The fact that direct labour costs sometimes do not vary directly with sales volume or production volume was referred to in Chapter 9. A small firm with four employees needs one more to increase production even by 10%. With five employees production may eventually reach 125% of present levels but to begin with the steep jump in direct labour costs is not moving directly with sales.

Between production volumes of 4 and 5 more direct labour is added causing the direct cost of production to jump out of direct relationship with the growth in sales.

The definition of direct labour is so imprecise and open to interpretation that care must be taken in comparing the results of one business with another. It does not matter greatly whether a business includes or excludes supervisory staff in calculating direct labour costs so long as actual and budget are calculated on the same basis.

The number of employees required for production emerges from the production forecast. Labour rates, allowing for annual or other increases, inflation, bonuses and overtime are then applied to the earning hours of the employees.

10.7 Indirect Costs

10.7.1 Production

Many of these costs are relatively easy to estimate. Where costs such as lighting are shared they can be allocated on the basis of the total area occupied by the production function, but beware of the accountability of managers mentioned in 10.5 above. Depreciation often causes problems because it is not as easy to identify with manufacturing activities as are repairs, renewals, power and light. Provision for depreciation has two functions: firstly, it charges activities (e.g. production) with an amount to reflect the benefit of using an asset: secondly, it reduces profit by setting aside an amount of money to make good the diminution of value due to its use and to provide for eventual replacement. The inflation rates of 1974 to 1976 showed that the amounts set aside were usually quite inadequate to provide for replacement. Inflation accounting may produce more realistic charges but, for the purpose of budgeting, a fairly aggressive depreciation policy should be adopted so that replacement is provided for over a short period and the activity is charged fully for its use of the asset. The point made above in the section on accountability is worth stressing. No manager can accept as a cost for which he is accountable one over which he has no control. Depreciation policy is usually decided at the highest level in any business.

10.7.2 Selling Expenses

The marketing or sales manager prepares a budget of costs – salaries, commission, expenses and advertising and promotion costs – necessary to achieve his sales forecast. Because of commission-related earnings the budgets will be flexible in amount. Small companies have little need for corporate image advertising since market shares are usually quite small. Any advertising should evoke direct response; even if cost budgets are not being exceeded the sales manager can cancel promotional campaigns if early results are disappointing. As with commission, these indirect support costs are very sensitive to changes in volume and budgets need to be fairly flexible. Beware of long-term sales efforts such as the high costs of establishing a presence overseas. Many small companies wait in vain for future business to recoup such costs.

10.7.3 Administration and Other

Interest costs can only be estimated if capital requirements have been calculated using a cash flow forecast (see Chapter 8). A cash flow forecast can only be prepared when some estimate of costs (including interest) has been made.

10.8 Action Points

1. Monitor variances and take corrective action.
2. Make managers accountable only for costs which they can control.

10.9 Forms

The specimen budget forms attached show how accountability for performance and costs can be allocated to the managers of the different functions. Even in a very small business, the owner/manager can find out exactly where he is doing well or badly by separating the different functions into different budget headings.

The Operational Budget (statement 1) shows that

1. The Sales Manager has responsibility for the sales budget. He may wish to delegate responsibility for sales performance to his area managers or to salesmen of a particular product (statement 2).

   His accountabilities include sales costs of £20,000 and £10,000 for administration (mainly telephone). A detailed breakdown of these costs would be shown on a separate budget form so that detailed reasons for variances could be ascertained.

2. The Production Manager is charged with producing a quantity of goods at the budget cost. He is responsible for the production overheads including supervisors' wages and repairs as well as the direct costs (wages and materials). A separate budget (statement 3) would be prepared. This budget would set out in detail the budget (in time and value) for achieving the production required in the budget period; the reasons for any overall variance in production costs could therefore be identified.

   Variances can be due to greater or less efficiency (i.e. less or more hours required than were budgeted for) or to unbudgeted changes in wage rates. The budget could be further refined by budgeting in detail for different groups of employees (e.g. by product line).

Cost Budgets

3   The Managing Director has responsibility for most administration costs (in larger companies this would be delegated to the Chief Accountant) and all other non-allocatable costs such as directors' salaries. Again the detailed costs would form part of a budget (administration budget – statement 4) where performance against budget could be monitored.

Operational Budget £000's

Statement 1

	Total	Managing Director	Sales Manager	Production Manager
Sales	500		500	
Prime Costs				
Direct Labour	150			150
Materials (adjusted for stocks)	200			200
	350			350
Overhead Expenses				
Production (per detailed agreed budget)	50			50
Sales (salaries, commission, expenses, advertising)	20			20
Administration (per detailed agreed budget)	20	16	2	2
Other (detailed – directors' salaries, audit fee etc.)	20	20	20	20
	110	36	22	92
Budgeted Profit Before Tax	40	(36)	478	(402)

Sales and Sales Cost Budget £000's

Statement 2

	Total		Area Mgr X		Area Mgr Y		Area Mgr Z	
	Bdgt	Actual	Bdgt	Actual	Bdgt	Actual	Bdgt	Actual
Sales								
Product 1								
Product 2								
Product 3								
Total Sales								
Overheads								
Salaries								
Commission								
Travel								
Entertaining								
Advertising								
Administration – telephone								
Total overheads								

Production Cost Budget

Statement 3

Period ended..................

Direct Labour	Hours Worked		Wage Rates		Cost		Total Variance	Analysis of Variance	
	Budget	Actual	Budget £	Actual £	Budget £	Actual £	£	Wage Rates £	Efficiency £
Overheads					Budget £	Actual £	Variance £		
Supervision									
Indirect Labour									
Lost Time									
Overtime									
National Insurance									
Holiday Pay									
Consumable Stores									
Maintenance									
Scrap and Rectification									
Depreciation									
Total Direct Overheads									
Total Labour and Overheads									

Managing Your Company's Finances

Administration Budgets

Statement 4

Department: Office Management
Manager: Period ended:

	This period			Cumulative this year		
	Budget	Actual	Variance	Budget	Actual	Variance
Number of staff						
Office Manager's office						
Secretaries						
Post room and messengers						
Telephone and Reception						
Total						
Expenditure	£	£	£	£	£	£
Salaries						
National insurance						
Holiday pay						
Temporary staff						
Sub total						
Printing and stationery						
Postage and telegrams						
Travelling expenses						
Repairs to office machinery						
Miscellaneous						
Total						

XI
Budgeted Profit and Loss

11.1 Introduction

Chapters 7 to 10 outlined an approach to Sales and Production forecasting and budgeting for capital expenditure and for direct and indirect costs.

The ultimate aim is the making of profit. When all forecasts and budgets have been prepared in draft a budgeted profit will result. If budgets are met this is the profit the business will achieve. Is it adequate? If not then the budgets must be revised to see if profitability can be improved.

Similarly, in a medium-sized business it is essential that a forecast balance sheet is constructed reflecting the achievement of the budgets. If the appearance of the balance sheet at the end of the budget period is unacceptable (e.g. stocks too high, borrowing too high) the budgets must again be revised.

Some small companies are just as concerned with the appearance of their balance sheet as with absolute levels of profits. A lender may have told them that borrowings must be reduced; to achieve this a lower scale of operation is necessary – lower sales, therefore lower debtors, lower stocks therefore less cash tied up – even though this may mean lower accounting profits.

The important point about budgeting is having an objective, be it profit (as in most cases), gearing (ratio of borrowing to assets), market share (unlikely and possibly disastrous for a small firm) or some other target. Budgets can be adjusted within achievable levels to reach these objectives.

11.2 A Practical Exercise

Mr. P. R. O'Duction is a manufacturer of components for major electrical switchgear. He has five basic products. He is nearing the end

Managing Your Company's Finances

of his productive trading year and can estimate the full year's results with some accuracy. His sales will be £500,000, net profits before tax £30,000.

11.3 Mr. O'Duction's Objectives

Mr. O'Duction is under no pressure from his bankers. His accountants have told him that he should be making a return on capital (net profit before tax related to net assets) of 15% but Mr. O'Duction believes in return on sales as a measure of success. He wants to go back to making profits which represent 10% of sales – a figure he achieved some years previously.

11.4 The O'Duction Budget

Mr. O'Duction begins his budgeting process. His order of budgeting and the headings are:

Sales Budget	Production Budget	1 *Materials Budget*	
		2 *Direct Labour Budget*	*Financial (or Profit) Budget*
	Capital Budget	3 *Indirect Costs Budget*	

11.5 Sales Budget

Mr. O'Duction's newly appointed sales manager is confident that he can increase sales revenue by 20% to £600,000. He can do this by cutting out one product, sales of which have been declining for some years, and stepping up the sales of two others which were introduced as new products two years ago and are already enjoying considerable market success. Sales prices will go up 10% across the board; it is expected that this will be in line with inflation.

Gross profits are arrived at by applying a standard material cost for each unit of each product to the volume produced in the year, adding direct labour costs (time sheets are kept for each production run) for each product and deducting the total direct cost from the sales revenue for each product. This gross profit expressed as a percentage of sales revenue gives 30% overall; the two new products have gross margins greater than this. There is no plan to launch a new product in the new year.

The draft sales budget is prepared:

Budgeted Profit and Loss

Product	Current Year Units	SP £	Value	Budget Units	SP £	Value
A	4,000	10	40,000	4,000	11	44,000
B	2,000	25	50,000	–	–	–
C	8,000	25	200,000	8,000	75	220,000
D	3,000	30	90,000	4,180	33	198,000
E	3,000	40	120,000	4,500	44	19,800
	£20,000		£500,000	£20,680		£481,000

11.6 Production Budget

No new accommodation would be needed but to cope with the substantial increase in production of products D and E a new machine at a cost of £20,000 would be essential. In addition one extra machine operative would need to be taken on. Without the machine the 40% and 50% increases in volume production of the high margin D and E products would not be possible.

11.7 Capital Budget

Mr. O'Duction produced a crude project cash flow (Chapter 4) and demonstrated to his own satisfaction that the machine would pay for itself in increased profits within three years. Products D and E now accounted for more than half of his turnover and nearly two thirds of his gross profit. He sanctioned capital spending of £20,000.

11.8 Materials Budget

With past experience of the material content of each product Mr. O'Duction, who looked after all shop floor operations personally, knew the current material cost of each unit. After adjusting for 10% inflationary price increases which were expected early in the new year he drew up his materials budget as follows:

Product	Quantity (per sales budget)	Cost Per Unit £	Total Cost £
A	4,000	5	20,000
C	8,000	9	72,000
D	4,180	12	50,160
E	4,500	16	72,000
	£20,680		£214,160

Managing Your Company's Finances

11.9 Labour Budget

Mr. O'Duction felt no need for a detailed calculation of standard hours. He controlled manufacture closely and knew how long each operation took. Because his employees did not have a high level of skill the likelihood that they would overrun on the time allocated for production runs was limited. Down time rarely occurred through human error; machine failure was the main problem.

Knowing, therefore, how many employees he had, adding the new machine operative, and allowing for a wage increase during the year Mr. O'Duction was able to calculate the total gross wage bill for the budget year. This totalled £165,840.

11.10 Indirect Costs

The company book-keeper took last year's production costs, adjusted for known increases in rent and rates and the cost of the new supervisor, added an inflationary 10% increase to the other items and passed the draft budget to Mr. O'Duction in his capacity as production manager. Total costs of £70,000, which included a depreciation charge on the proposed new machine, were agreed.

The sales manager prepared a list of the costs of his department. Including commission, which would be payable if sales reached £600,000, and an advertising campaign costing £20,000 to back the drive on the products D and E, his budget totalled £70,000.

Administration expenses and other costs, as adjusted for 10% inflation, totalled £45,000 including increased interest charges following the machine purchase.

The Indirect Costs Budget in total were:

Production	70,000
Sales	75,000
Administration	45,000
	£190,000

11.11 Draft Financial Budget

This is the resulting budgeted profit and loss:

Sales		£600,000
Materials	£214,160	
Labour	165,840	380,000
Gross Profit		220,000
(36%)		

Budgeted Profit and Loss

Overheads	190,000
Budgeted Net Profit	30,000
Required Net Profit	60,000
(10% of sales)	
Shortfall	£30,000

11.12 Budget Revision

The existing budgets do not meet the stated objective – a profit of 10% on sales, or £60,000. The results show the same profit as last year which now represents only 5% of sales instead of 8%, and this despite an increase in gross margin from 30% to 36%.

Mr. O'Duction re-examined costs. His production costs having risen little from the current year, he looked at the sales department where budgeted costs were three times the current year's estimate of £25,000. An analysis was made:

	Current Year £	*Budget* £
Sales Manager (including car)	–	15,000
Salesmen (3)	18,000	30,000
Expenses	7,000	10,000
Advertising	–	20,000
	£25,000	£75,000

The advertising budget was discussed. The company had never advertised before but the sales manager, who had come from a large company, had used advertising in other jobs to boost the effort of salesmen on the ground. After discussion it was agreed that because of the nature of Mr. O'Duction's customers, who were mainly large original equipment manufacturers, the advertising was unlikely to bring in new business or help convert existing enquiries.

The commission rates were clearly too generous. Salaries increase 67% while sales increase 20% (10% through price increases). The growth in sales of D and E is 40% and 50% respectively but the salaries increases represent 10% of the increase in these sales. The commission rates were adjusted to reduce earnings to £22,500 at target levels and expenses cut to £8,500 to achieve Mr. O'Duction's profit of 10%.

11.13 Action Points

1 Set clearly defined objectives.
2 Compare budgeted profit with objectives.
3 Revise budgets (e.g. indirect costs) to achieve objectives.

Objectives

Mr. O'Duction's checklist would look like this: What do I want to achieve this year and in the long term?

Sales

1 How will national (and international) economic conditions affect sales?
2 How strong is the order book? To whom am I going to sell additional production?
3 How are current sales holding up and what is the trend?
4 Will competition affect my sales forecast?

Production

Have I the capacity to produce the goods required to meet the sales forecast? Do I need more plant or storage space?

Materials

Are materials readily available? Are any price increases forecast and can these be passed on to customers?

Labour

What manning levels will I need? What wage increases are likely? Will the increased production mean bonuses, overtime?

Indirect Costs

Which costs will increase as activity increases? Are there any true fixed costs? Have I adjusted for inflation and known future increases in costs (e.g. power)?

Are there any increases in staff required to cope with additional administration loads?

Reconciliation

If the financial budget does not meet my objectives can I:

Budgeted Profit and Loss

1. Reduce overheads and where?
2. Increase margins without losing volume or vice versa?
3. Change the sales mix or drop a product line to increase gross profit contribution?
4. If I cannot, is my objective realistic?

XII
Pricing

12.1 Introduction

Most textbooks on marketing begin by stating the four 'Ps' which are the key areas when selling a product or service:

Product (or service) — Quality, design, packaging.

Promotion — Advertising, organization of sales team.

Place — Availability, delivery.

Price

An examination of the first three is outside the scope of this book but pricing plays a vital part in ensuring that sales and profits are achieved. Some large companies, where a market is dominated by two or three producers, let prices find their own levels but concentrate hard on the three other 'Ps'. This chapter concentrates on pricing.

Before embarking on a pricing strategy, the small businessman must decide what his objectives are. In Chapter 11 Mr. O'Duction was not interested in improving the look of his balance sheet; he wanted to make a return of 10% on sales. The objectives may be profit-based or market-based. (They can of course be based on a desire for a quiet relaxing life but this chapter assumes a more aggressive attitude).

12.2 Profit-Based Objectives

These are usually:

1. To make a target return on sales or capital in the short (or long) run.
2. To make reasonable profits (enough to keep the bank manager or

Pricing

outside shareholders happy but not enough to incur a large tax bill).
3 To maximize profits (in the long run or the short run).

12.3 Sales-Based Objectives

These are usually:
1 To increase sales (which does not necessarily mean increased profits).
2 To hold on to existing market share (a very difficult aim to achieve).
3 To increase market share (perhaps at the expense of profit).

At the outset the small manufacturer or trader should not accept that he has to allow the market to dictate prices. If there is a clear market leader a framework of pricing may exist but this should not deter a smaller producer from considering a different structure. If competition was perfect the market leader's price would prevail. However small companies can often cater for minority tastes or beat the market leader in other areas – a better developed product, better delivery or better salesmen and after sales service. These advantages can command a premium price.

12.4 Variable Pricing

With a fairly standard product it is simple to charge one price to all customers. Charging a uniform price is particularly common in retailing, although the value of individual goods is different to different customers. Because the price level is well known, competition can offer similar products at lower prices.

The problem with selling the same products at different prices is that the customer who pays the higher price may find out about the others, prices may take longer to negotiate because the customer is aware that there is flexibility and salesmen often give way on price to close a sale. The control of pricing and profitability could become very difficult if much variation was allowed.

Small businesses make much use of discounts in varying prices (see chapter 5).

12.5 Discounts

12.5.1 *Volumes or Quantity Discounts*

The cost of processing a large order for standard products is relatively

Managing Your Company's Finances

less than that for a small order. Part of this additional profitability can be passed to the customer to encourage a sale.

12.5.2 Trade Discounts

Deductions from the price offered to the public give retailers their margin; further deductions give wholesalers their margin. This is a delicate area. If distribution of products is arranged through wholesalers, supplying direct to retailers undermines the wholesalers and may have the long-term effect of destroying market presence. There are many recorded examples of manufacturers simplifying their discount structures by supplying direct to the public or the retailer only to regret it later; the distributors (wholesale or retail) charge margins for a service. The margin cannot be earned either by the distributor or the manufacturer without providing that service.

12.5.3 Seasonal Discounts

The retail trade's 'January sales' are a traditional feature but manufacturers with high (costly) stocks could usefully employ this tactic from time to time provided it did not upset the market. Smoothing the levels of sales means even efficient production, minimum stocks and a better cash flow.

12.5.4 Cash Discounts

This improves cash flow at the expense of profit (see Chapter 5). Although cash discounts can be used effectively to reduce prices to a cash-rich customer, often discount levels are standard in the trade and every customer will expect a certain level of discount for an early payment.

12.6 Setting the Price

There are two basic approaches to the setting of prices: cost-based pricing and market-based pricing. The first approach to be considered is cost-based pricing.

12.6.1 Cost-Based Pricing

All costs need to be considered including an arbitrary allocation of overhead on the basis of expected operating levels.

The most elementary method is mark-up or 'cost plus' pricing. Cost plus is usually found where costs are difficult to 'cost' in advance, such as construction or, in some service sectors, agencies supplying temporary staff.

Pricing

In the case of an employment agency, a figure per man-day of qualified staff is charged. This provides the agency with sufficient income to pay the employee, overheads and direct expenses and have a margin for profit. The method takes no account of competition, the willingness of the customer to pay the price, and the fact that the cost might depend on the price because it will affect volume. In practice the customer is willing to pay for the immediate availability of staff. The alternative is carrying surplus labour.

With Government contracts or assignments for large institutions the price can be fixed on actual cost plus an agreed small margin. This protects the supplier from escalation in costs and the customer from excess in profits being taken out of the contract. Most Ministry of Defence contracts are on this basis and the rules on what is allowable are laid down in detail.

There are two basic methods of costing:

a) Absorption Costing, where overheads are recovered by applying a percentage to prime cost (or some other 'direct' base). If activity is greater than expected, overheads will be over-recovered because they do not increase with levels of activity. The product is therefore charged out at a much higher profit than expected, but may not sell because of overpricing. The reverse, where activity is too low to recover overheads, may result in losses.

b) Marginal Costing measures the amount by which total costs change if output is increased or decreased by one unit. The break-even chart in Chapter 10 showed the effect on profit of increases in sales where only variable costs increased. Management can examine the gross margins on each product (see table 12.1) and choose to discontinue lines with loss gross margins or 'contributions to overheads'.

There is a great deal of controversy about the two methods of costing. Management need to decide for themselves which is more appropriate for their business. The main points in favour of absorption costing are:

i) A comparison of one production profitability can only be made if all costs are included. The exercise in 12.1, therefore, can be dangerous.
ii) Marginal costing needs a recovery rate to absorb variable overheads.
iii) Selling prices cannot be determined without full costing.
iv) Closing stocks contain an element of fixed costs which are part of the costs of production.

The points in favour of marginal costing are:

i) Over- and under-recovery of overheads is avoided.
ii) Absorption costing does not show actual costs.
iii) Fixed costs should not be carried forward in closing stocks. These costs are incurred in a given period and should be written off.
iv) Where output is greater or less than forecast, the effect is clear and there is no problem with changing unit costs as fixed costs are not charged to production.
v) As marginal cost measures profitability and the ability to cover fixed costs, it is a better management control system.
vi) The effect of changes in sales mix is apparent.

Managers must think carefully about long term effects before taking action particularly on the basis of marginal costing information.

12.6.2 Market-Based Pricing

This can be based on the value to a customer of goods or services and involves variable pricing (see 12.4 above). It also takes account of the price he is able and willing to pay for the goods or services. Businesses using this approach develop special (i.e. non-standard) products or services which command premium prices.

The other market-based approach is to price on the basis of what competitors are charging. Although this approach was not supported earlier in this chapter it could be defended on the grounds that 'follow my leader' is a substitute for reliable knowledge of how the market would react to price differentials, that it is less disruptive to industry harmony and that, where costs are difficult to measure, the going rate is the conventional wisdom and should yield every supplier a reasonable return. Unfortunately the cost structures of small companies and market leaders are likely to be radically different. A good example of competition-based pricing is the bidding system in the contracting industry. Prices are pitched low enough to beat competition; thus the expectation of competitors' pricing levels is apparently more important than detailed costings.

12.7 Factors to Consider

The factors to be considered vary depending on the type of business. Three basic types should be examined:

1 Services.
2 Distribution.
3 Manufacturer.

Pricing

12.7.1 Services

The greater the materials content the more the pricing will be cost-based rather than market-based. Thus servicing/maintenance of washing machines will be cost-based while the 'pure' service of professional advisers (solicitors, accountants, consultants) will be marked-based. The material costs or expenses (e.g. travelling, typing) would be charged separately from the professional fee.

Standardized services such as dry-cleaning are highly competition oriented. There is little that is non-standard and competition would quickly seize a price advantage. Costing will determine the lower limit of prices.

Where services are customized or unique, prices are based very little on competition or costs but largely on what value the customer puts on the service and what he will pay. Examples could be top consultant surgeons or tax experts who may charge a basic fee plus a percentage on tax saved. In the area of uniqueness high prices often indicate quality of service, even if the latter is unproven to the customer.

Prices for services can more easily be varied to suit individual customers without causing problems in the market place. Since the quality of service can also be adjusted it is advisable to price high enough to be able to sustain good service. The service should be improved from a standard one to a speciality one by differentiating it from those of competitors and so commanding a premium price.

The provision of a speciality service requires in-depth knowledge of the explicit needs of the customer and the development of refinements to the standard service to meet these needs. Customers will pay a premium price if they really get the service they want.

12.7.2 Distribution

The distribution industry covers every business distributing goods – mainly wholesalers and retailers. Most pricing is cost-based. The manufacturer takes his manufacturing costs and adds a mark-up for profit when selling to the wholesaler. The wholesaler breaks bulk, that is, splits the large consignments of goods from the manufacturer and distributes to a number of retailers having added a further mark-up to cover his costs and leave him some profit. The retailer adds a further mark-up to cover his costs and profit in pricing to the customer.

Mark-Up

The mark-up used in distribution depends on whether the business is wholesaling or retailing. In comparing these it is interesting to use manufacturing mark-ups as a yardstick.

Managing Your Company's Finances

Manufacturer

The mark-up is a percentage added to cost. Thus if manufacturing cost is 67p the manufacturer may sell to the wholesaler for £1 – a mark-up of 50% (33/100 × 100/1) on prime cost or a gross margin of 33% (33/100 × 100/1). The manufacturer will have £33 from every £100 of sales to cover indirect costs and provide profit. Costing/Pricing by manufacturers is looked at later in this chapter but it should be noted that manufacturers often add a small profit margin to total costs including overheads (rather than direct or prime costs).

Wholesaler

The wholesaler takes the £1 article and, for his stocking and handling costs and his profit, he adds a 20% mark-up to his bought cost and sells to the retailer at £1.20. Note that the manufacturer, who is adding considerable value to the raw materials, has much greater indirect costs and is carrying stocks for a long time, puts on a large mark-up. The wholesaler adds much less value but provides a service by storing, holding stocks available and finding outlets. He may also add some value by repackaging goods delivered in bulk in a form which is more easily handled by retailers and possibly more aesthetically appealing.

A small mark-up of only 20% is appropriate considering the low value added. However, the wholesaler is handling large amounts of stocks and the stocks move very quickly. If a wholesaler allows the movement of stocks to slow down his margin will be insufficient to prevent losses. (In this case the gross margin is 16.7% (20/120 × 100/1).

A wholesaler can increase his prices and margins by providing greater service. For example a steel stockholder has a slower stockturn than a chemical sundriesman. Quantities of steel are held locally so that the stockholder has to finance the stock and act effectively as banker to local engineering companies. He may also decoil steel, cut it to size and even give advice as well as selling ancillary equipment.

Retailer

Margins here vary. The local dress shop or ironmonger's store may take the £1.20 article from the wholesaler and add about one-third for a mark-up. This gives a selling price of £1.60 and a gross margin of 25% (40/1.60 × 100/1). This may appear a high gross margin compared with the wholesaler's. However the local ironmonger may carry stock for three to four months while the wholesaler may have stockturn of 12 (that is every month, on average, stock is completely

Pricing

sold and replaced). By holding stock, albeit in smaller quantities, for longer, the shopkeeper is providing a service to the public. Moreover he provides premises where customers can get advice about the right type of screwdriver or how to clear a drain and have the facilities to view merchandise only a few minutes from their own home. The local quality dress shop may have even higher mark-ups because it provides changing rooms, knowledgeable assistants, quality shopfittings and services such as guaranteed exchanges or money back.

The retail trade has been undergoing great changes in the last twenty years or so. The three 'Ps' of Place (convenient location), Product (specialists in certain lines), and Promotion (local goodwill) allowed local corner shops to have slow stockturns compensated for by relatively high mark-ups. The growth of supermarkets (less convenient, non-specialist standard ranges of products but perhaps better promoted in the professional sense) began a trend towards faster stockturn, higher turnover and much lower gross margins (much lower than 10% on most food lines). Recently, discount stores and hypermarkets have appeared. These are, at first sight, less conveniently located and are non-specialist and offer no services such as advice. What they do offer is lower prices (very low margins) and they have very high stockturns. In fact location is now found to be convenient; consumer habits have changed to weekly grocery expeditions to remote locations where cars can be parked easily and shopping done quickly.

The multiple stores often now buy direct from manufacturers, taking the wholesale profit as well as the retail, and specialist departments (e.g. gourmet foods) are appearing in very large stores. The small retailer still has some convenience of location. He has to struggle hard to provide additional services to match the price disadvantage which he can do little about. Keeping open longer hours, stocking specialist lines, delivering to the house and making shopping a more pleasant and human experience than a visit to a supermarket can still allow gross margins of two or three times those earned by the larger stores.

Finally, these comments on retailing mark-ups ignore the fact that not all three have the same stockturn. Mark-ups on fast moving lines can be lower because the product of volume and margin gives profit. The reciprocal can also be true. A lower mark-up can increase sales. Thus a range of products may have a range of mark-ups.

The build up of the selling price to the end customer can be shown as in Figure 12.1.

From the original manufactured (prime) cost of 67p the mark-ups have increased the ultimate selling price to £1.60.

Managing Your Company's Finances

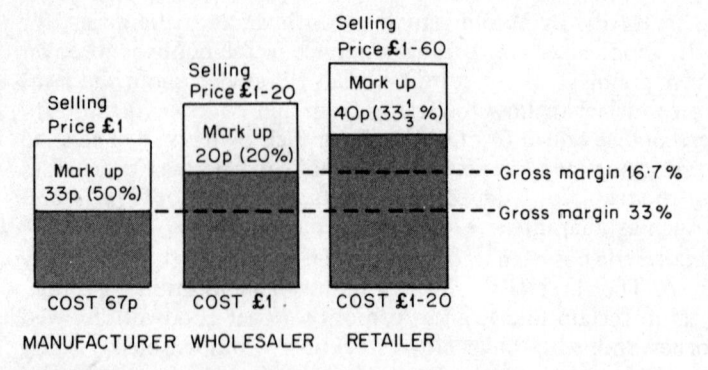

Figure 12.1

Manufacturer: Cost 67p, Mark up 33p (50%), Selling Price £1
Wholesaler: Cost £1, Mark up 20p (20%), Selling Price £1-20
Retailer: Cost £1-20, Mark up 40p (33⅓%), Selling Price £1-60
Gross margin 16.7%
Gross margin 33%

12.7.3 Manufacturer

a) Cost-based Pricing

Earlier in this chapter the practice of 'cost plus' (similar to mark-up pricing) in construction was mentioned. The problem for a manufacturer, in using 'cost plus' pricing, particularly with standard products, is that some costs vary directly with volume level of output and sales and others do not. The total cost per unit of producing 10 units compared with producing 100,000 units is clearly enormous. Yet too often businesses price on the basis of the year's cost per unit of production. In Chapter 10 the difference between fixed and variable costs and their effect on profits was demonstrated by a break-even chart.

It is not satisfactory for a manufacturer to use cost-based pricing alone. Wholesalers and retailers may handle a wide range of products. On some they make profits, on others losses, but overall the uniform mark-up they apply can prove profitable (as well as simple). The manufacturer can price on the basis of Mr. O'Duction's budget in Chapter 11 but this takes no account of the market demand for his products. The rest of this section considers the effect of demand on pricing. It is assumed that, in a small business, standard machine-hours or man-hours for given levels of output can be calculated without undue difficulty and that overheads which are indirect or largely fixed in nature can be calculated on a square footage basis or by some reasonably acceptable method. On the basis that prices which cover fixed and variable costs can be determined – how should this be applied to the real market?

Pricing

b) Demand and Supply

The break-even chart in Chapter 10 suggests that increasing profits are available at increased levels of production and sales. This is fine, provided the market will continue to buy. There is an economic theory, marginal utility, which comes into play. A man may be prepared to pay 20p for an orange, even 40p for two if he is keen on oranges. To buy four or six he may need a small reduction in price but it is unlikely that he will buy eight or ten for his own consumption, even if the price is reduced substantially. The extra oranges are no value to him, there is no marginal utility. Similarly it is not possible to sell into a market more than it will find a use for. If demand was totally 'elastic' – that is if customers would continue to take any quantity of goods at a given price – then pricing would be unnecessary.

Assume that quantities and prices in Table 12.1 produce the incomes shown.

Table 12.1 Marginal Revenue

Quantity	Price (£)	Total Revenue (Quantity & Price) (£)	Marginal Revenue (£)
0	100	0	–
1	80	80	80
2	70	140	60
3	60	180	40
4	50	200	20
5	40	200	0

Table 12.1 shows that the additional revenue from selling one more unit is small and can even be negative at high quantities (6). The total revenue is perhaps satisfactory when selling 5 units but the total revenue is just as great if only 4 are sold. There therefore seems little point in increasing sales in a market where demand is such that to do so requires price reductions which produce a negative or poor level of marginal revenue. The question is – what is the relationship with marginal costs? If the variable costs of producing each additional unit are looked at against the additional revenue produced by selling each additional unit, the effect of greater sales on profit is more realistically shown than in a break-even chart.

The unit variable costs involved in producing the first (additional) units in Table 12.2 are obviously high and the total marginal cost is

Table 12.2 Fixed and Variable Costs

Quantity	Total Fixed Cost	Average Fixed Cost	Total Variable Cost	Average Variable Cost	Total Cost	Average Cost	Marginal Cost Per Unit
1	30	30	10	10	40	40	40
2	30	15	15	8	45	23	5
3	30	10	20	7	50	17	5
4	30	8	25	6	55	14	5
5	30	6	35	7	65	13	10

therefore high. The marginal cost of producing additional units settles down to a steady £5 and in theory should stay there. The cost of making and selling very low levels of production is high, but economies of scale come into play until a point is reached in all small businesses when the costs of additional sales (per unit) begin to rise again, partly due to the cost of the additional selling effort. Products can no longer 'sell themselves' above certain levels of output. The average cost of each unit continues to fall or levels out but the marginal cost of each additional unit has begun to increase. In fact, fixed costs are rarely fixed at higher levels of production as is suggested here.

Taking the appropriate columns for Tables 12.1 and 12.2 the effect on profit can be seen in Table 12.3.

Table 12.3 Marginal Profit

Quantity	Total Revenue	Total Cost	Total Profit	Marginal Revenue	Marginal Cost	Profit
1	80	40	40	80	40	40
2	140	45	95	60	5	55
3	180	50	130	40	5	35
4	200	55	145	20	5	15
5	200	65	135	0	10	Loss 10

This shows clearly the result of reducing prices to obtain additional sales which cost relatively more to make. There is a substantial marginal loss on the fifth unit.

12.8 Summary

There are no simple action points which can be set down for this chapter.

Pricing

There is no magic formula for pricing. Questions about what level of sales might be achieved at given prices can only be answered by those in close touch with the market. The answers must always be subjective but without those answers, no assessment of marginal revenue can be made. The marginal cost of sales can only be estimated by an analysis of fixed and variable costs along the lines of Mr. O'Duction's budget in Chapter 11. Standard labour or machine hours for units of production must be arrived at and standard material cost per unit must be calculated. Fixed costs are not always fixed and indirectly variable costs sometimes move up more sharply at higher levels of output. When marginal costs are compared with marginal revenue the broad range of prices can be determined. From there on, trial and error within a range which is known to yield the greatest profit will allow the small company to find its true pricing level.

In pricing its products and services the small business must decide:

1   Is the product or service cost-based or market-based?
2   How can the product or service be differentiated to increase the mark-up or gross margin?
3   What is the marginal cost of, and the marginal revenue arising from, selling additional goods or services?

Much of this chapter may seem theoretical in the extreme to small businesses. Yet often too little thought is given to pricing in small businesses. In 12.6.2 above, the 'follow-my-leader' approach was shown to have some appeal. Managers of small businesses should seek as much guidance as possible, from trade associations and statistical surveys, and can use agents to price for them.

A price can only be determined if it is known what the product is and at whom it is aimed; in this respect the points covered in Chapter 9 are relevant.

XIII
Justifying the Raising of Finance

13.1 Introduction

In this chapter the raising of finance is discussed. Later chapters are concerned with the types of finance available and the sources of such finance. The emphasis here will be on presenting a case to an external source of finance. The importance of such presentation cannot be too strongly stressed as poor presentation is the most common weakness of applications received by lending organizations.

The chapter deals particularly with the two main aspects of raising finance, namely justifying the requirement within the company and then persuading an outside source to provide the finance. The viewpoint of the institution is also discussed in the hope that some insight into the way such bodies look at applications may help companies in their presentations.

13.2 Basic Considerations

It should be obvious that any consideration of a project which may require additional finance needs to be made against the background of up-to-date accounts. If the risks of a new venture are to be properly considered and if the working capital requirements are to be accurately calculated, it is vital to be fully aware of the current state of the company's profitability and cash flow. This is particularly important when an external source of finance is approached, as much of its deliberations will centre around the strength of the company's current and forecast trading position.

A lender will expect to see recent audited accounts and will prefer to see up-to-date monthly management figures. If the previous year-end audit is not complete, an estimate which will bear investigation or

Justifying the Raising of Finance

which will be borne out by subsequent audited figures will usually suffice but an approach from a company whose audited accounts are, say, two years behind, does not impress. Some companies find themselves faced with a dilemma when they first approach an external source of finance if they have convinced themselves in the past that the latest possible date of filing of their accounts will be beneficial for tax reasons. This argument has become weak over the past few years as the Inland Revenue may now make an assessment of what they consider should be the tax, on which interest will become payable from the due date regardless of whether accounts have been filed. Furthermore, in recent years very few companies have paid Corporation Tax anyway because of stock relief provisions. Unfortunately it is, in our experience, too often the case that the late production of audited accounts is more likely to be attributable to sloppy financial control and inadequate auditors than to a carefully thought-out policy which will produce real benefits.

The previous chapters have discussed financial control of a company and the importance of budgets. Any provider of significant amounts of finance to the company will wish to be satisfied that finance controls are sound and the company's forecasts will be at least as, if not more, important to the lender than its historic accounts because it is the future profits which will service finance, not the historic trading. Historic trading does, however, serve as very useful evidence of the company's quality and often significantly underpins the credibility of the forecast.

In summary, the first step to take when considering the raising of new finance is to make sure that full and accurate financial information on the current and forecast performance of the company is available. Only when this base information is available can a case for further finance be properly prepared.

13.3 New Project Forecasts and Internal Considerations

Much of what follows specifically relates to the raising of finance for new projects rather than, say, additional working capital to finance increased turnover or balance sheet restructuring. If finance is not required for a new project, the considerations become somewhat simpler but should follow the same general pattern and the contents of an application to a lender will be much the same.

13.3.1 *Project Forecasts*

Having conceived a new project, be it a new factory, a new product or an acquisition, very careful consideration will have to be given to the detailed commercial and financial aspects. Some of these considerations may prove difficult. For example, it is hard enough in most companies to forecast the sales of established product lines and forecasting the sales of a new product may prove almost impossible. It is important to be conservative in these forecasts as the emphasis will probably need to be on avoiding large losses in the early stages rather than making large profits. Again it must be recognized that, however thorough the market research may be, most new ventures require a high degree of faith in addition to careful preparation.

Difficult though they may be, these forecasts, perhaps prepared in conjunction with the company's professional advisers, are the essential preliminary to the further considerations. Examples of cash and profit forecasts are given in Chapters 4 and 11 respectively.

13.3.2 The Amount of Finance Required

The cash flow forecast and capital budget for the project should show how much finance will be required in total and distinguish between the permanent need for the project and the more transitory working capital aspects. It should be noted that it is disastrous to under-estimate requirements and can be expensive to over-estimate them. This underlines yet again the importance of good forecasts but if an error is to be made it is better to over-provide finance than to be caught short at a crucial moment. A loan to be drawn down only if and when required would avoid paying for unnecessary finance yet can guarantee the availability of sufficient finance to cover contingencies.

The next stage is to decide how much of the finance can be provided from internal resources, which again requires the basic accounting and forecasts discussed in 13.1 above. The answer to this question may not be obvious. It may be possible to exercise a stricter credit control within the company, thus collecting debts more quickly and releasing cash. It is possible that suppliers can be persuaded to give longer credit without penalties, although if medium-term finance is required, this source of finance needs to be viewed with caution. Other cash economies may result from a careful re-appraisal of the level of stock or work in progress and, finally, the expectation of retained profits from the company's future trading should not be forgotten. Careful re-appraisal of all these matters should result in a well-defined requirement for any external capital.

13.3.3 Other Considerations

Of the other matters which need to be considered, the most important are the implications of the project in management terms. It is

Justifying the Raising of Finance

essential, if a project is to succeed, that sufficient management time should be devoted to it. This may require changes in the job responsibilities of existing management, increased delegation to subordinates and further recruitment.

It is also worth remembering that legal and tax considerations can sometimes be important. It is an unfortunate aspect of the current taxation system that tax is often a major parameter in discussing the real profitability of a project and may sometimes be the deciding factor in the question of whether or not to go ahead. The danger of assuming that the current tax legislation will remain unaltered throughout the duration of a project should be noted.

13.3.4 Returns and Risks

By this stage it should have become clear whether or not the project is profitable, after taking into account all costs including those of external finance. However, profitability alone is not sufficient justification for proceeding. The return on the capital employed, i.e. profit before interest compared to the total capital employed, should be examined, particularly if other projects are mooted and only one can be carried out. This concept is discussed in more detail in Chapter 8. If the company is not deciding between several alternative projects, when a high priority is usually given to the rate of return on capital, the discussion to proceed or not will centre around whether the potential profits from the project justify the risks of proceeding. Chapter 3 discusses this concept in more detail.

The risks must be considered with care. Many companies do not pay sufficient attention to them and there are countless tales of subsequent woe which could have been avoided if a project had been more carefully considered at an early stage. One advantage of approaching a source of external finance is that a second opinion on the risks of the project will be available and criticism from such a source should be welcomed. In any event, if the project is particularly risky a company is unwise if it does not seek the opinion of its professional advisers who should be capable of giving a more dispassionate view than any member of the company's management who has become closely, and perhaps too closely, involved with the project. As an extreme example it is most unwise to consider a project which, if it goes badly, will hazard the very existence of the company itself. This may seem obvious but many companies have failed for this reason.

One example of failure we have seen was a London-based dress manufacturer which wished to expand by moving from leasehold premises to large second-hand freehold premises. In the event budgets proved to be very far from accurate, due to difficulties with the local authority over building regulations, increases in cost of imported plant because of exchange rate changes and some deliberate increase in the specification of refurbishments. Constant delays increased costs further and finally losses were incurred because of management time being spent on the problems with the move at the expense of normal duties. Although the company did move into the premises its cash difficulties did not ease and the erosion of assets by losses added to inadequate financial information meant that the bankers felt unable to increase their support and a receiver had to be appointed. Failure can be attributed to incorrect budgeting, inadequate financial control and insufficient management in depth to cope with the ensuing losses.

Most of the risks of a project will relate to either the ability of the company to achieve the necessary sales forecasts, its ability to commission plant or its ability to control the overheads. One common project which is much more risky than most companies appreciate is a manufacturing company's move to a new factory. In our experience such a move almost inevitably costs considerably more than is budgeted and some companies fail as a result of the ensuing cash crisis. This underlines the importance of very careful planning and the necessity for sufficient contingency in the available cash resources to cover unexpected difficulties.

13.3.5 Internal Presentation

It is vital that all members of a company's management who will be involved in subsequent implementation are behind a new project. The manager who has done most of the preparatory work on the project is likely to be the person with the highest degree of commitment and it is important that his ideas are fully criticised in a formal board meeting before the decision to proceed is taken. Only at this stage is the company ready formally to approach an external source of finance, although it may already have had informal discussions with its existing providers of finance in the early stages of the conception of the project.

13.3.6 Professional Advisers

It has already been mentioned that a professional adviser has the advantage, as a critic, of a lesser degree of involvement with the project. He should therefore be capable of objective criticism. In addition his professional skills as, say, an accountant may prove invaluable if the company is considering issues which are somewhat unfamiliar to it.

A professional adviser who is behind the project can then often

Justifying the Raising of Finance

serve as an excellent presenter of the case for support to a provider of finance. Indeed, through his professional contacts he may well be able to make preliminary introductions to suitable providers and, from his previous experience, be capable of advising the company on the institution's investment policy.

13.4 Time Scale

If you are intending to approach an institution for a significant amount of finance which may involve considerable financial risk for the institution, it is important to allow ample time for your application to be processed. Of its very nature long term finance carries an implication of careful planning and no institution will be impressed by an urgent request unless there is very good reason for it. The degree of involvement and risk implied by some applications means that an institution will quite properly require a few weeks in which to make up its mind. This is not a bureaucratic requirement but arises from a necessity to investigate thoroughly such applications and, indeed, to crystallize the thinking of the lending executives who need to go through many of the same thought processes that the company executives have already done. There are, of course, always instances where applications will become urgent with good reason. However, it should be borne in mind that if the application is very marginal the imposition of a tight deadline is likely to lessen its chances of success.

13.5 Security

Before discussing the presentation of a case to a source of finance it is worth looking at some of the ways in which such an organization will view the security (in both capital and income terms) available to it.

13.5.1 Capital Security

It is almost axiomatic that any lender of finance will look for the best security available and that its terms will reflect its own view of the quality of that security. The most concrete security, if not necessarily the most saleable, is normally seen as freehold or long leasehold property. It must be expected that the major provider of finance and certainly any long-term lender (see paragraph 14.2 regarding the concept of matching) will first look to any bricks and mortar which the company has. It is also not uncommon for balance sheet values of property to be very much out of date and valuation therefore becomes of importance. Before lending against the security of property, any lender will wish to be satisfied with its value and may wish to instruct his own valuer for this purpose.

Although property is normally regarded as the best form of security, it must be recognized that special purpose buildings or property in unusual locations can be very difficult to value on an alternative use basis which will result in a very conservative figure being produced by any professional valuer. Also, a commercial lender will not normally regard property as security for a loan of more than, say, two-thirds of its value. The difference between the size of the loan and the value of the property is designed to cover the arrears of interest which are almost inevitable if foreclosure occurs, particularly because of the period of time which it may take to sell the property (for commercial property a year is not uncommon).

In suitable industries other items of fixed assets are often acceptable security. Particularly good would be, for example, standard printing machinery for which there is always a reasonable market. Any very specialized or immovable items of plant will not normally be considered to have good security value.

The current assets are of most interest to a short-term lender such as the bank. The reason for this is that as debts to the company are settled, the money is paid into the bank account and automatically reduces the overdraft. A long-term lender will be less enthusiastic about debtor security as the debtor figure could be seriously eroded long before he attempts to recover his money. In normal circumstances a bank lending on debenture security will usually require, say, a two or three times multiple of debtors compared with the loan. This reflects the risk that some debts may not be good, that the total debtor list may have been eroded before repayment is sought and that a number of items including certain PAYE and wages can become preferential to creditors secured only by a floating charge. An organization taking specific security on each acceptable debt (which applies to invoice discounting or factoring) would usually be prepared to give considerably higher percentage advances against such security.

The other major item which appears in current assets is stock and work in progress. Its value as security depends greatly on the industry. Any organization which is selling bought-in finished goods will have stock which is reasonably readily realizable and can therefore form good security. On the other hand, a manufacturing company may have its stock mostly composed of raw materials and part-finished products, neither of which is very valuable in a liquidation.

In addition to examining the assets in the balance sheet (some of which may be charged to others) a lender may be interested in seeking security from assets outside the business. A common way of taking

Justifying the Raising of Finance

such security is to take a personal guarantee from directors. A more restricted version of this is to take a specific charge on certain realizable personal assets such as an investment property.

The security available from the assets of the business will be one of any lender's major considerations. There are ways of compensating for security which is less than perfect and these include a premium interest rate or an element of the loan convertible into shares. However, capital security alone is not sufficient for the majority of lenders.

13.5.2 Income Cover

In addition to capital security a lender will normally look closely at the profitability of the business and its ability not only to pay interest (which is tax deductible) but also to repay capital (which is not tax deductible) over the agreed period.

This is the reason for a close interest in the company's profit and loss account and cash flow forecasts. Most lenders will expect to see a reasonable safety margin between the company's projected profits and the costs of servicing a loan. If the servicing of the finance depends upon a forecast increase in profit the lender will need to be satisfied that this forecast can be achieved.

13.5.3 Other Considerations

One concept which is frequently used by institutions to describe the security risk is that of gearing. Although defined in a number of ways, this is most usually taken as the ratio of total borrowings to the net asset value of the business. Gearing gives a crude indication of the degree of capital security available, in that high gearing implies there are relatively few assets available to distribute amongst the various lenders. In addition, and more importantly, it gives some indication of the degree of risk of the company not being able properly to service its total borrowings. The concern here is the degree of safety margin in the profit level of the company before interest charges compared with the interest charges themselves. It should be noted that not only may profitability fall for all the normal commercial reasons but that if a highly geared company is entirely dependent on variable rate finance, the interest charges may change dramatically as market rates alter.

As a broad generality a company will frequently be regarded as highly geared if the ratio exceeds 1 to 1. Many companies, particularly small and rapidly expanding ones, are geared much higher than this but it is worth studying the balance sheets of a few listed companies as their gearing levels are typically considerably lower than this.

13.6 Presentation of Your Case

If anything other than a very simple form of finance is sought the lender will require to know a great deal about the company in general and the proposition in particular. Most lenders are only too happy to discuss matters informally at a preliminary meeting but they will always be more impressed if reasonably full information is supplied prior to that meeting. Individual lenders will vary in the detailed information they require but, as an example, here is a list of suggested preliminary information published in one of ICFC's brochures; this list is typical of other institutions' requirements.

Presenting Your Case

A general guide to the information which it is helpful to receive for the first meeting.

1. The amount of money sought, and how it will be used.
2. Products or services – standard publicity handouts and sales literature are very helpful.
3. Names of directors and senior management with ages and experience.
4. Information on current trading, e.g. draft accounts for a full or part year.
5. Audited accounts for five years or, if the business has been trading for less, the full trading period.
6. Forecasts, including general budgets and cash flows and specific project budgets where appropriate.
7. Major shareholdings and particulars of any long term debt.
8. Names of bankers, with overdraft and security arrangements.

Once the company has completed its own internal planning and decision-making process and has prepared preliminary information, it is ready to approach a lender. If the company's professional adviser has been involved in the preparation and planning, he is an obvious person to invite to the preliminary meeting and as he may have more experience of what the proposed lender will be looking for, he can be a valuable contributor to that meeting.

13.7 What the Lender is Looking For

Any potential lender will wish to ask a lot of questions before making a decision on your proposition. Most institutional investors will also insist on visiting your premises to gain a closer feel of the business and how it is run on a day-to-day basis. First impressions are important, as

Justifying the Raising of Finance

such people are usually busy men who are considering many applications at any one point in time. Their impression will probably depend very much on how well thought-out the proposition is and how the questions are answered.

Once the lender has full details of the proposition he can complete his assessment of it as a potential investment. It is worth remembering that, whatever form his investment takes, he is looking for the return of his money in one form or another at the end of the day. This makes his approach very different from that of a salesman who is, for example, selling office equipment. The lender will be seeking to establish the following:

1. Confidence in the management of the company and in particular in the key individuals.
2. Confidence in the business or proposed business. In the case of an established company this may easily be established with a summary of historic accounts. In the case of a start-up it will depend on market research and a great deal of other investigation.
3. Confidence in the use to which the money will be put. This must appear to make sound commercial and financial sense and not to involve too high a degree of risk for the company.
4. Confidence in the security. If a secured loan is sought, the key to this will be the value of the assets offered as security. The other important aspect is that the lender will wish to see the borrower with sufficient of its own finance at stake. In the case of a company this is largely a simple comparison between the weight of proposed borrowings and the net worth of the business. In the case of a start-up or purchase of a business, it will be a function of how much finance the applicants are themselves putting up relative to the finance requested and, more importantly, what their degree of commitment is – which includes how much they stand to lose if the project fails.

All the above features are important to the lender but the order of priorities will, to a large extent, depend on the particular situation being considered. However, once institutional support is required which involves long-term loans or equity there is no doubt that most investors would consider the quality of the management of the business to be of the greatest importance. In a long-term investment situation the historic accounting and current value of the company's assets are certainly some guide to the long-term security of the investor's finance. However, if the investor is to be involved for ten, fifteen or more years, all features of the business can change dramatically and it therefore becomes of the utmost importance to believe that the company's management will be capable of adapting to economic change and of continuing to guide the company towards profitable expansion. The extreme example of this situation is where, for example, an organization is asked to buy a minority stake in the equity of a private company for tax planning reasons. Such an application usually is aimed at ensuring a family company remains in the family hands for at least another generation. Thus the investment is of almost indefinite length which means that the institution becomes interested not only in the present management but also in the provisions that have been made to ensure management succession as older members retire.

13.8 Raising Money in Times of Crisis

Many companies experience crises at some stage in their development and such crises often result in a shortage of finance leading to an emergency application to an external source. This is undoubtedly the most difficult type of application to prepare and the one with least chance of success.

If help is sought from a commercial lender, success depends on persuading the lender that the crisis can be overcome. Profit and cash flow forecasts are thus crucial as is assessment of the management's ability to overcome the crisis. It is important that, if the crisis has occurred whilst the company is under its existing management, credible explanations are provided of how the crisis occurred and why it will not recur.

It is not impossible to raise finance in such circumstances and Table 15.1 (see page 000) indicates the institutions which will consider such applications. Often the problem with an application of this type is that the company's management has been, or is, deficient in certain respects. Many companies who have got themselves into trouble recognize this point and it is increasingly the case that investing institutions will consider applications from companies that will be viable provided additional finance and additional management support is available. In recent years there has been a recognition that certain propositions are only viable if additional professional management support is provided. It seems likely that the trend to providing such assistance in particular cases will continue.

13.9 Common Weaknesses of Propositions

The most common weakness of all is that of inadequate preparation and presentation of the application for finance. It may not be

Justifying the Raising of Finance

important when an institution's views are first sought that an application has been prepared in detail. Indeed many institutions welcome a first informal meeting prior to a formal approach. However, once that formal approach is made, the institution expects the potential customer to have thought through his application in detail and to supply the necessary financial details.

Apart from a general inadequacy of preparation, the commonest most specific failing is that of an inadequate allowance for contingencies. It is normally better to have more finance available than might be required if all goes particularly well, to allow for problems. However, it is sensible to have a facility for the contingency which does not incur interest charges on money which might not be required. A bank overdraft automatically provides this and long-term loans can often be drawn down only as required.

In our experience of looking at companies, the commonest weakness is that of poor financial control. Any long-term lender is very concerned about the future ability of the company to survive and to adapt to a sometimes rapidly changing world. Efficient accounting systems and strict control over cash flow are vital if the company is to avoid unnecessary risk. There is no doubt that many small companies are deficient in this respect.

13.10 Summary

This chapter has above all emphasized the need for careful preparation and presentation of any application for finance. No lender will be impressed with a poorly prepared application and first impressions are important.

It is thus essential that full consideration of the proposed project and application be made within the company before a lender is approached. This consideration must include the availability of management time for and commitment to the project.

Finally all applications should include up-to-date accounting information and, often, forecasts of the future performance. The satisfactory preparation of this information is only possible if the company has proper financial and accounting systems.

13.11 Action Points

1 Prepare full and accurate information on the current and forecast financial performance before seeking finance.

Managing Your Company's Finances

2 Prepare forecasts on a conservative basis. Allow for contingencies and make sure money requested is sufficient.
3 Make sure of management commitment to a new project and allow for the demands of this on management time.
4 Seek a second opinion, preferably from a professional adviser.
5 Do not take risks which threaten the company's existence.
6 Allow time for a lender to process an application properly.
7 Remember that a judgement of management ability is the most important part of the assessment of an application for finance.
8 Remember that the most common weakness of applications for finance is inadequate preparation.

XIV
Types of Finance

14.1 Introduction

In this chapter we discuss the types of finance which are available to the owners of a business. This is a subject which has often been written about but most of such work has concentrated on shorter-term financing. For this reason we have chosen to emphasize the features of longer-term financing as well as to discuss the type of finance appropriate to a particular business need. A consideration of the types of finance available will be a necessary part of the financial resource planning process and a company's plans will need to be considered in detail before the precise amounts of external finance are decided upon.

14.2 Capital Structure

Because of the severe constraints on management time, financial resource planning of the smaller business is often neglected. Although this is not an easy discipline, it leads to control and can create a stable financial base for growth. Cash forecasting and the establishment of a good blend of short, medium and long-term capital form part of the financial plan. The basic essentials of a sound balance are well known. The principle on which this is based is to keep the life of assets and their relevant financing of similar length. This is known as 'matching'.

Using the matching principle, working capital should be provided from short-term (renewable) sources of cash, usually in the form of bank overdrafts which represent the most flexible source of short-term capital. Medium-term investments (e.g. vehicles and plant with a restricted life) are generally suitable for hire purchase, leasing or medium-term loans. Longer term investments (over five years) such as buildings, heavy plant, some working capital and capital for acquiring

Managing Your Company's Finances

other companies, should be financed from shareholders' funds (share capital and retained earnings) or from long-term loans (see Table 14.1). It is particularly important that in times of inflation companies plan their cash requirements well ahead. It can be very costly and sometimes impossible to raise cash at short notice under conditions of desperate financial need.

Historically, the smaller business has paid little attention to its capital structure. It has tended to grow from within its own resources and from bank overdrafts. Only when the bank reached its lending limit would the smaller firm seek alternative sources of investment capital; in other words its search for finance became forced rather than planned. The result has often been that firms have borrowed 'short' and invested 'long', and in times of recession their lower levels of profits and cash flow have led to a reduction in bank lending. A cash crisis often resulted. In recent times these problems have been exacerbated by unprecedented rates of inflation which have forced many firms to raise increasing amounts of working capital to finance a level of turnover which has not been increasing in volume terms.

14.3 Availability of Finance

The majority of businesses are well aware of the availability of short-term finance, most forms of which are provided by clearing banks. Medium and long-term capital is more readily available than many small/medium sized companies realize. Risk-bearing capital in the forms of ordinary shares, preference shares and unsecured loans can be obtained from a number of sources. Convertible loans and long-term borrowings are more commonly available, but the smaller business has often been either ignorant of the whereabouts of their sources or reluctant to undertake such commitments. The decision to borrow capital from sources other than bank overdrafts is not easily made and is often rejected without due consideration. To appreciate the range of finance available it is helpful to look at their uses, advantages, disadvantages and costs.

14.4 The Types of Finance and Their Uses

Table 14.1 summarizes the broad types of finance, their uses and sources.

14.5 Short and Medium-Term Capital

This type of finance is frequently written about and a number of reference works will give most of the information on the subject which

Types of Finance

Table 14.1 Matching Sources of Finance to Uses

Type of Capital	Uses	Matching Asset	Sources
Short-Term (up to 3 years)	1 Working Capital	Stock, debtors	Bank Overdraft
	2 Financing seasonal fluctuations		Bills of Exchange
	3 Financing export orders		Letters of Credit
	4 Bridging finance		Creditors
	5 Minor fixed assets		
Medium-Term (3–7 years)	1 Financing fixed assets	Vehicles, plant and fittings	Medium-Term Loans
	2 Working Capital	Stock, debtors	Hire Purchase, Leasing
Long-Term (7–20 years)	1 Financing assets with long life	Freehold and long leasehold property. Plant and machinery	Redeemable Preference Shares
	2 Permanent working capital	Permanent stock or debtor requirement	Long-Term Loans
Permanent	1 Broaden borrowing base		Share Capital
	2 Financing major fixed assets	Freehold property Long leasehold property	Retained Profits
	3 Financing acquisitions	Shares of acquired company	

you might require. The advantages and disadvantages of this type of finance are included in the general summary in Table 14.2

The simplest and most common form of short-term financing is an overdraft facility which is normally available for general use by the borrower. Most other forms of short-term financing relate to specific transactions such as large orders or the exporting of goods. These include bills of exchange, invoice discounting and letters of credit. Factoring is a more general form of invoice discounting which will often include servicing of the sales ledger. When used it is usually as an alternative to a bank overdraft.

The common forms of medium-term financing are (1) a medium-term loan from a bank which again has general application; (2) hire purchase; and (3) leasing. Hire purchase and leasing are increasingly used for the purchase of assets such as plant, fittings and motor vehicles.

Table 14.2 Comparison of Types of Finance

	Description	Advantages	Disadvantages	Costs
1	*Bank Overdraft (from Clearing Banks)*			
	Most common form of borrowing. A borrower is allowed to let his bank current account become overdrawn within certain limits.	Usually cheapest finance available; flexible; quickly obtainable; no minimum sum; interest paid on usage only; normally renewable; can sometimes be unsecured.	Technically repayable on demand; highly vulnerable to change in Government and banking policy; temptation to use for wrong applications (because of cheapness, and convenience); may require personal guarantees.	Floating interest charge at Base Rate + 1 to 4%; commitment fee may be charged in certain circumstances.
2	*Short Term Loan (from Clearing Banks and Finance Houses, often owned by Clearing Banks)*			
	More formal arrangement than overdraft. Lender agrees to advance a sum for a period of months.	Term commitment by lender; cheap rates often obtainable from finance houses in return for HP business; often quickly obtainable; sometimes unsecured; can often roll over; improves overdraft flexibility.	Dearer than overdraft (except in special circumstances); uneconomical if funds not really required; probably requires security in situation where overdraft would not; may involve some restrictions.	Floating interest charge at BR + 2 to 5% may be fixed at 2 to 4% cent above corresponding short gilt yield; probably legal costs plus possible negotiation fee.
3	*Credit Factoring (from Specialist Finance Houses, often owned by Clearing Banks)*			
	Finance is provided against each specific invoice. The factor will advance, say, 80% of the value of the invoice. Usually the factor operates the company's sales ledger for a fee and collects the debts as they fall due.	Can save costs if properly used – but often doesn't; credit linked to sales; used properly can be very convenient over a bridging stage; flexible; factors may carry bad debt risk (for extra payment). High percentage advance.	Can be some loss of contact with customers; difficult to terminate service; tendency to become over-dependent on service; regarded by some financiers as sign of weakness; might reduce overdraft facilities; dearer than it looks at first glance; minimum invoice/account value £100/£1,000 puts it beyond reach of some who need it most.	Floating interest charge at BR + 2½ to 4% plus administration charges of 1 to 2% of invoice value.

(cont.)

Description	Advantages	Disadvantages	Costs
4 Invoice Discounting *(from Specialist Finance Houses)*			
A form of factoring where each invoice is discounted by the finance house i.e. it lends, say, 80% against the security of the invoice. However, the operation of the sales ledger remains with the company.	No loss of contact with customers; can be ended easily; credit linked to sales; flexible; not so expensive as credit factoring; inexpensive and fairly quick to arrange; can be great help in tight liquidity situation.	Might reduce overdraft facilities; tendency to become over-dependent on service; dearer than overdraft facilities; regarded by some financiers as a sign of weakness.	Floating interest charge at BR + 2½ to 4%.
5 Hire Purchase *(from Specialist Finance Houses, mostly owned by Joint Stocks Banks)*			
The company hires the equipment from the finance house for a fixed period *and* has an option to buy at the end of the period for a nominal sum. Legal title (and hence capital allowances) are the company's from the outset. Deposits of 10% to 30% are common.	Quick and inexpensive to arrange; ideal for short life, heavy use assets with guaranteed return, costs and repayment terms fixed for period; does not normally affect bank overdraft (peddled enthusiastically by most bank managers); capital allowances available straight away; not classed as borrowings.	Fairly expensive; terms subject to Government regulation (but never in retrospect); default may be prosecuted over-vigorously; interest expressed as flat rate can be misleading (rule of thumb for contract under two years double flat rate to get true rate).	Interest fixed at equivalent of around Finance House Base Rate + 4% at time of negotiation.
6 Leasing *(usually from same Finance Houses as do HP)*			
In contrast to HP title never passes to the company which leases the equipment until such time as it is worthless or is sold. No deposit is usually paid.	Same advantages as HP except since ownership does not pass, capital allowances are not available to lessee except through terms of lease.	Ownership does not pass, therefore no capital allowances.	Roughly same cost as HP – though examine net present value of before and after tax cost as compared with HP.

(cont.)

	Description	Advantages	Disadvantages	Costs
7	*Acceptance Credits Bill Finance (from Accepting Houses)*			
	A form of invoice discounting but with only specific transactions being financed.	Cheap; flexible; ideal for financing specific short transactions without affecting overdraft arrangements.	Apparent sophistication frightens off most small businessmen; little dearer than overdraft finance.	Fixed interest rate at three months rate + 1½ to 4% plus 1 to 1½% commission.
8	*Medium Term Loans (from Specialist Financial Institutions, Clearing Banks, Merchant Banks, Government and EEC Sources)*			
	Formal arrangement to provide finance (usually secured) for a period from 3–7 years.	Term commitment by lender – costs and repayments known ideal for financing fixed assets; low minimum sum from some sources; inflation lessens real cost.	Might involve borrowing and other restrictions; dearer than shorter period finance; early repayment may invoke additional interest charge on amount of anticipated redemption.	Fixed or floating interest charges – floating at six months Inter-Bank Rate + 1½ to 4%; fixed subject to negotiation; negotiation fee likely plus own legal costs.
9	*Long Term Loans (from Specialist Institutions like ICFC, Insurance Companies, Government and EEC Sources)*			
	Usually secured. Finance lent for 7–25 years.	Improves financial flexibility; other advantages same as for MT loans; improves balance sheet; cumulative effect of inflation renders this highly economic in real terms.	Same disadvantages as MT loans; insurance company loans dearer than they look when linked to life policies; lengthy to arrange (allow four months); may be partly convertible into equity.	Fixed interest rate negotiable at the time – depends on going long-term rate; negotiation fee plus own legal costs.
10	*Sale and Leaseback (from Property Companies, Insurance Companies and Pension Funds)*			
	Finance source buys the property from the owner/occupier and leases it back to him. Ownership may then change hands but tenant has obligations under the terms of the lease (see below).	Term commitments by lenders – costs known. Provides a source of equity at almost comparable cost depending on the yields for property at the time.	The sale of the property removes a source of security for future borrowing. Rent reviews may be frequent and rapidly increase the cost of raising the initial finance.	The costs are fixed; legal costs will have to be paid and there may be a tax liability due to previous application of roll-over relief.
11	*Share Capital (from Specialist Institutions, Merchant Banks, Pension Funds)*			
	See 14.5.	Improves the borrowing platform and net assets. Dividends are appropriation of profits.	Can be expensive and, if in equity form will water the existing equity.	Depends upon the class of shares and circumstances of the case.

The above Table is reproduced by kind permission of *The Accountant*.

14.6 Long-Term and Permanent Capital

Whilst short and medium-term finance is often written about, long-term and permanent capital as financing methods appear to be less well understood and are worth looking at more closely.

14.6.1 Long-Term Loans

(a) *Security* will reflect the length and therefore greater risk in lending, compared with short-term. Such loans are usually secured on the assets they finance – freehold and leasehold property and fixed plant. If these assets give insufficient cover, a floating charge on current assets, ranking behind the company's bankers, is often looked for. The loans are seldom unsecured in the smaller business and negative pledges (e.g. not to fall below a given current assets/liabilities ratio) are not common. Restrictions on some activities such as further borrowing are, however, quite usual.

(b) *Interest* rates are usually fixed in contrast to most short and medium-term lending, reflecting the way in which the lending institutions raise such money.

(c) *Repayment* over seven to twenty years can be made in a variety of ways – equal periodic instalments, e.g. quarterly, half-yearly or annually; smaller repayments in the early years and larger ones in the latter ones; equal periodic payments of a varying mixture of interest and capital such as the building societies use. Some institutions will grant a 'holiday' i.e. no capital repayments for the first few years. Insurance companies often use endowment funding schemes using policies on the life of young directors or partners. The nominal interest rates on such loans are generally a few points lower but the effect of life assurance premiums which are not allowable for Corporation Tax must be considered.

(d) *Convertible Loans.* These are sometimes used where security is inadequate or where the income cover is in doubt. The lender usually has the option for a fixed period to subscribe money for new shares at a price fixed at the outset or by a formula. If the option is exercised, the subscription money is used to reduce the loan.

(e) *Early Repayment* of fixed rate loans can mean the payment of additional interest to compensate the lender for interest forgone. This gives some protection to the lender in event of sharply *falling* interest rates when his own fixed rate borrowings are not repayable; the borrower has total protection against *rising* interest rates. A variable rate loan usually carries a smaller or no early payment penalty reflecting the fact that the lender is reborrowing his money at period intervals.

14.6.2 Preference Shares

These are shares usually issued for cash and carry rights to a fixed annual dividend. On a sale or liquidation of the company they are normally repayable at a fixed sum. In other words they have no 'equity' in the proceeds but they are repaid preferentially to the equity shareholders. Also, in contrast to most equity shares, they rarely carry votes except in certain specified situations such as dividends being in arrears by six months or more.

(a) Irredeemable shares usually carry a higher fixed coupon than redeemable shares. A premium on the redemption of redeemable shares is common.
(b) The effective cost must be considered. As dividends are paid out of post tax profits the comparable interest rate (which is tax deductible) is approximately doubled if the company pays Corporation Tax at 52%.
(c) Variable or participating dividends, linked to profit levels, can substitute for or supplement fixed dividends.
(d) They are still considered to be gearing, though a more permanent form of finance than loans.

14.6.3 Equity

Subscription of cash for equity by new shareholders dilutes the holding of all existing shareholders. Purchase of equity from one or more shareholder puts cash into shareholders' pockets and leaves the other shareholders unaffected.

There are many types of equity shares. Two of the more common are:

(a) Ordinary Shares

Institutions are usually only interested in ordinary shares if there is a proven and progressive dividend policy or a very likely chance for capital gain on realization in a few years. Individuals on the other hand, because of high tax rates on income, may be quite happy with ordinary shares. The opportunities for realization through obtaining a listing are not frequent and, with a few notable exceptions, institutions are not interested in very long-term holdings especially if the dividend yield is low. Institutional policy on board representation, valuation of the shares ('an art not a science'), dividend requirements and minimum size of investment vary a great deal. An institution is

Types of Finance

usually particularly concerned with the running of the company, board representation, the way in which it sees itself realizing its investment and its attitude to further issues of shares and changes in dividend policy. This can be even more important where a large block of shares is being placed with a number of institutions.

(b) Convertible Preferred Ordinary Shares

These overcome the problem of individuals and institutions taking different views of dividends. A new class of share (which can be non-voting if issued for cash) is issued with the shares carrying the right to fixed dividends or in some cases a dividend linked to profits. Dividends need not be paid on the ordinary shares. Thus the institution through its holding of preferred ordinary shares meets its dividend requirements without obliging the ordinary shareholders to take dividends which, for tax reasons, may be unattractive to them. When converted into ordinary shares the right to the dividend is lost and the shares become indistinguishable from the rest of the ordinary shares.

14.7 Stock Market Listings

A stock market listing as a method of raising finance is really beyond the scope of this book. Publications such as *Going Public* (by M. J. Richardson) and booklets produced by members of the Issuing Houses Association go into the subject in detail.

There are problems for a small company which in practical terms needs £1 million of pre-tax profit to contemplate a listing. At the time of writing, the cost of an issue is in excess of £200,000 and in some cases nearer £300,000. Even a small rights issue would not cost less than £100,000. Often the cost of accounting investigations and advertisements in the Financial Times account for half of this figure. For the raising of, say, £1 million this cost is prohibitive.

One advantage is said to be that there is a market in the shares. Many small companies which floated in the late 60s and early 70s found that the after-market in the shares was very thin and an attempted sale of, say, 5% of the equity depressed the share price considerably. The ability to make an acquisition on a share for share basis can, however, be a considerable benefit.

The Unlisted Securities Market (USM) has been developed to provide a method of achieving marketability at relatively low cost. The USM arrangement will, for actively traded stocks, virtually replace trading in unlisted securities through brokers under Rule

163(2) of The Stock Exchange. The cost of a USM listing is in the range of, say, £40,000 to £90,000.

In the USM only 10% of the equity (not 25% as with a full listing) need be made available to public. At the time of writing there are more than fifty companies listed on the USM. This market is probably not appropriate for companies earning less than £200,000 net pre-tax profit.

Substantial private companies wishing to raise equity can arrange to place minority stakes in the ordinary shares with major institutions. Fees are around 1/1½% of the amount raised. A dividend on the amount raised will have to be paid but there is unlikely to be interference in the day-to-day management of the company.

14.8 Government Support

In addition to the commercial sources of finance the Government is a substantial provider of money for business.

14.8.1 UK

This varies depending on whether the company is in a Special Development, Development or Intermediate area, though certain industries can receive support regardless of situation. The subject is huge and cannot be summarized here. Booklets are available from the Departments of Trade and Industry. Help is available not only in the form of Interest Relief, Regional Development and other grants and loans but also through the capital allowance tax structure. Government agencies such as the National Enterprise Board, Welsh Development Agency and Scottish Development Agency can provide equity and loan finance and CoSIRA specializes in financing firms in rural areas. There are Government financed 'advanced factories' in some depressed areas and many local authorities have schemes for providing accommodation and cheap loans to attract industry.

14.8.2 Europe

European Investment Bank foreign currency loans with a UK Government exchange risk guarantee are available for capital investment in Development areas. The attraction is a lower rate of interest than is available from commercial UK sources.

European Coal and Steel Community sterling loans at low fixed rates are available where jobs are being created for redundant coal and steel workers. British Steel Corporation can also provide financial help in this connection.

Types of Finance

14.9 The Pros and Cons of Different Types of Finance

The advantages and disadvantages of the various broad types of finance already discussed are summarized in Table 14.2. In practice, a company needs to consider its particular requirements carefully before it can attach the correct weight to each advantage or disadvantage and the final decision may often be a compromise. One obvious conclusion is that too much emphasis on cheapness may necessitate the taking of risks which in the longer term can prove disastrous for a business. Long-term money, be it loan or shares, is seldom cheap but does result in a sound capital structure and in many cases, perhaps more importantly, greater peace of mind. It is a foolish man who, having spent years building up a business, risks its eventual survival to save a percentage point or two of loan interest.

14.10 Summary

In this chapter we have attempted to draw your attention to the many different types of finance which are available to even the smallest business. As a company grows it will need to consider its capital structure from time to time, to ensure that it remains soundly based at all times and that the shareholders are not running financial risks which may not be apparent on first sight.

Once the requirements for external finance are no longer simple, the subject becomes complicated and many factors need to be considered. The final result is often a compromise and it is important to realize that, if an outsider is asked to invest his money in a company in a way which involves increasing risk for him but decreasing risk for the company, this will almost certainly increase the cost to the company. However, avoiding the increase in cost by continuing with an unsound capital structure may prove to be very false economy in the longer term. There are in addition many occasions when a company is obliged to improve its capital structure because commercial lenders will no longer continue to increase their lines of credit until the situation is improved.

Once again the importance of planning in considering all the issues carefully has been emphasized. When this exercise is complete it is necessary to find a suitable source of the required finance and this is the topic of the next chapter.

XV
Providers of Finance

15.1 Introduction

The previous chapter discussed the many types of finance available to a company. The importance of a sound capital structure was emphasized and some of the difficulties of making a final decision about types of finance were mentioned. An additional difficulty is that any potential provider of finance will have its own views and the final decision on how to structure any external finance will depend on agreement between the company and the source of such finance.

Historically, the smaller business has tended to be ignorant of the many potential sources of finance available to it. We hope that a better appreciation of these sources has resulted from the increase in publicity which was stimulated by the recent political interest in smaller businesses. This chapter attempts to give a reasonably full list of the sources of finance and a small amount of information about the likely requirements of each such source. Inevitably the list cannot be exhaustive and it is intended only to serve as a guide to the possibilities.

Having found a possible source of finance the company must also consider whether or not that institution's policy towards its customers is acceptable. One particular example of this may be the importance of whether the institution wishes to appoint a director; many companies feel strongly on this point. Another important point may be the institution's policy regarding the timescale of the future realization of any shareholding it may take.

15.2 Sources of Finance

15.2.1 Existing Shareholders

In a private company the shareholders are often also the directors of that company. Thus not only are they the eventual recipients of any dividends or the sale proceeds of the company but also their very livelihood depends upon it. For this reason the degree of commitment is normally great and provided such individuals have finance available they can often be persuaded to invest more in the business through additional share capital or loans. As such individuals will be receiving benefits through salaries and the potential capital gain of their shares they can also often be persuaded to invest money at little or no direct cost to the company.

The weakness of this source is that most families who own private companies have almost the whole of their assets, possibly built up over many generations, locked into the company. In the long term this is not a wise policy as there are many reasons which could cause a company to fail and wipe out carefully acquired wealth almost overnight. Indeed with the increasing burden of taxation related to the transfer of assets from one party to another it is essential that the owners of such a business have some liquidity in order to meet capital transfer tax. Thus it can be argued that in the long term a family should gradually dis-invest from its sole business and spread some of its investment risk elsewhere. If the family wishes to retain control of the business it has three ways of achieving this. Firstly, it can repay any directors' loans. Secondly, as the business increases in strength it should attempt to avoid personal guarantees to the bank which put assets outside the business at risk. Finally, it is possible to sell minority stakes in the equity to institutional buyers or to the public through some form of share quotation.

15.2.2 Individuals

Not so long ago it was common for members of a family to provide money to help the younger generation start or expand a business. This money was almost always risk finance i.e. shares or unsecured loans, against which further finance could be obtained from a bank, and was often cost-free. Unfortunately in recent years tax legislation has become such that this source of finance is increasingly hard to find. The Wilson Committee acknowledged this fact and christened the problem 'the Aunt Agatha Gap'.

Despite the decrease in personal liquid wealth it is still possible to raise finance from individuals. Increasingly however it is necessary to look further afield than the family. An almost inevitable consequence of investment by an outsider is that he or she will require shares in the business, a seat on the board and an effective partnership in the overall running of the business. Such an offer therefore needs very careful consideration because of its far-reaching consequences. Indeed, although new money from an individual may well appear cost-free in that loans are interest-free and any share subscription may

Managing Your Company's Finances

be for ordinary shares, it is often a fairly costly transaction. The individual may require significant director's remuneration, an expense account and a car. Finally, an individual is not usually a good source of further finance.

Despite all these qualifications, an individual can sometimes be a sensible source of finance, particularly if that person has professional skills or contacts from which the company can profit. In addition, there have been recent tax changes to encourage individuals to finance young companies.

15.2.3 Clearing Banks

The clearing banks are by far the major provider of finance to businesses. The majority of their finance is short-term and is dominated by the standard overdraft facility. However, banks offer a very wide range of products (over 200 from the majors) and are increasingly moving into longer-term lending. The main facilities available from a clearing bank are as follows:

(a) Overdraft.
(b) Medium and longer-term loans – the interest rate is normally variable and the majority of such financing is for periods of less than seven years.
(c) Hire Purchase and Leasing – these are usually provided by a subsidiary of the main bank.
(d) Factoring and invoice discounting.
(e) Export Credits Guarantee Department finance – in conjunction with the Government-backed ECGD the bank can arrange insurance and finance for export transactions.

A small business will almost inevitably first raise external finance from a clearing bank. At an early stage in a company's development it is likely to require overdraft finance to cope with short term fluctuations in its cash needs. Whilst the bank may take security on the assets of the business from the outset it will almost always insist on a personal guarantee, reflecting the poor asset cover in the early stages. It is, indeed, common for banks to ask for personal guarantees from the directors of almost any private company though they will not always insist that these are given.

The next stage of development, which is to seek finance from an institution which can offer longer-term loans or an equity package, is a less obvious and easy step. This sometimes means that a company operates for too long with overdraft finance being its only source of external capital. The directors should always be conscious of the risks of raising all finance from one external source. The temptation to

Providers of Finance

prolong these risks may increase as the banks themselves move further into longer-term financing.

15.2.4 Merchant Banks

The merchant banks are a useful source of finance for the larger private company. They tend not to be interested in small financing propositions and £100,000 is a common minimum level. They can often be persuaded to help with consortium deals and are a useful source of professional advice. Much of their financing is short-term, e.g. invoice discounting, but long-term financing also is often available.

15.2.5 Insurance Companies

The insurance companies can sometimes be a useful source of long-term finance. They usually prefer to lend for fifteen to twenty years and are normally only interested in mortgages. It is common for such finance to be linked to endowment policies secured on the lives of the younger directors or partners and the cost of the non-tax-allowable premiums must be considered in addition to the interest rate. They tend to be one-shot lenders (i.e. they are not interested in further financing) and a further disadvantage can be that the insurance company's first charge on the company's main asset, its premises, may reduce the possibility of raising further finance from elsewhere.

15.2.6 Government

The Government is a very useful source of cheap finance and a wide range of grants and loans is available. However, the availability of these facilities is constantly changing and the latest literature must always be consulted.

Some further comments on this source are given in paragraph 14.6 and brief details of the main Government agencies are contained in Table 15.1.

15.2.7 Institutional Sources of Finance

Table 15.1 summarizes the main institutions operating in the private company market at the present time. The table gives very brief details of the types and amounts of finance which each of these institutions will provide and, through the size of its portfolio, gives a guide to its presence in the market place.

15.3 Choosing Your Source

The advantages and disadvantages of using individuals and clearing banks as sources of finance are discussed above. The possible

Managing Your Company's Finances

problems with individuals are easy to appreciate but the pitfall of putting all your eggs into one basket and raising all external finance from a clearing bank is less obvious. The difficulty is that the problems will not become apparent until times become hard for either the company or the bank. It is thus easy, though fallacious, to argue that as in the past the bank has always provided all the finance required and has never asked for a decrease in the facility, there is no need to look elsewhere for finance. The depression of the early 70s did, however, bring this problem home to a number of companies.

If institutional backing is sought, a difficult question is how to decide between institutions. At one extreme, the proposition may be so difficult to persuade an institution to back that it will be necessary to approach a number in order to obtain any kind of offer. However, a sound business which is carefully planning its future should not be faced with this particular dilemma. Its dilemma will rather be which institution is best suited to its needs.

Certain institutional features are clear. Some will always require a non-executive director on the board, others seldom do. Some have a very definite policy regarding the length of time they are prepared to be involved in the company, others do not. Some can offer a wider range of additional facilities than others and some have very different views on the rate of return they expect on their investment. These and other similar factors are easy to establish and may well dictate which institutions to approach in the first place. Much of the rest of the decision is likely to rest on the details of the package offered by different institutions and the efficiency and style with which they handle the application. The most important point to remember is that, with the possible exception of a straight loan, long-term packages are reasonably complicated and are difficult to unwind. It is therefore vital that the company chooses an institution with which it will be happy to have a continuing relationship over the years to follow.

15.4 What Does the Institution Expect?

The way in which to present an application to an institution has been discussed in Chapter 13. The importance of the company choosing its institution carefully has also been mentioned. However, it is also necessary to recognize that institutions do themselves have expectations about the future behaviour of their customers.

The cardinal rule is to keep the institution fully informed of the company's progress and problems. This is particularly helpful when the company has future financing plans as the institutional view of

Providers of Finance

such plans can be sought at an early stage which may save considerable abortive effort. It is vital that an institution is aware of potential trading difficulties if a sympathetic approach to a crisis request for finance is required. Finally, it almost goes without saying that if a company wants its institution to treat it fairly, it must reciprocate. No institution looks favourably upon a customer who does not pay interest or dividends on the due dates without good reason and previous discussion. A further application for finance is unlikely to be welcomed if the company has proved itself to be a difficult payer.

15.5 Summary

Three points which have been made in this chapter deserve emphasis. First, the possible sources of finance which are available to the private company are more numerous than is often realized. Secondly, there are long-term dangers in raising all external finance from one source. Thirdly, if institutional support is required, the decision is an important one as the majority of long-term packages involve a high degree of commitment between the two parties and institutions vary enormously in their investing policy and after-care requirements.

Many of the comments in this chapter refer to the pitfalls of raising finance from external sources. However, there can be enormous benefits and there are many instances of companies which, with the frequent injection of institutional funds, have gone from strength to strength and at a greater pace than would ever have been possible from within their own resoures.

15.6 Action Points

1 Remember there are many more sources of external finance than is commonly appreciated.
2 Beware of becoming dependent on any one source of finance.
3 Choose your sources with care; long-term finance involves a long-term relationship.
4 Remember the source of finance has its own views on how to structure the finance and its own future expectations from a company.
5 Remember to keep a lender fully informed at all times.

Table 15.1 Sources of Finance

Where to go when the bank manager says 'no'

Vehicle for Capital	Backers	Capital earmarked	Type of client or situation	Min/Max funds injected	Start up capital	Rescue capital	Equity stake	Seat on Board	Term of funding	Exit criteria	Special features	Portfolio
Barclays Development Capital Tel: (01) 600 9234	Barclays Bank Group	Open	Established growth companies earning £100,000+ pre-tax	£100,000+ minimum, but may syndicate large investments	No	Exceptionally	Yes, 10–40%	Yes	Open	Flexible	Able to formulate equity/loan packages in co-operation with Barclays branches	3 companies – £1.1 m
Capital Partners International Tel: (01) 629 9928	Private European Investors	Open	Companies with overseas expansion potential	Up to £350,000 may syndicate larger investment	Yes, if exceptional overseas potential and convincing home management	By backing and/or introducing new management	Yes	Yes	Open	Flexible to suit company and other shareholders but expectations of long term involvement	Management assistance and overseas marketing development	10 companies – 5 in UK, 5 overseas – £1.1 m
Castle Finance Tel: Norwich (0603) 22200	Norwich Union	Open	Profitable private companies requiring capital for expansion	£30,000–£500,000	Exceptionally	No	Yes, up to 30%	No	Medium and long term loans – fixed or variable interest	Looking for dividends: sale of equity when convenient to all shareholders	Supplementary financial services of the Norwich Union Group	Group holdings – 35 companies – £3 m
Charterhouse Development Tel: (01) 248 3999	Charterhouse Group	Not disclosed	Mature and/or swiftly growing companies	£50,000–£5 m	Exceptionally	Only within portfolio	Yes	Yes	Open	To suit company and shareholders	Financial skills and experience	66 companies – £10 m

(cont.)

Vehicle for Capital	Backers	Capital earmarked	Type of client or situation	Min/Max funds injected	Start up capital	Rescue capital	Equity stake	Seat on Board	Term of funding	Exit criteria	Special features	Portfolio
Commercial Bank of the Near East Tel: (01) 283 4041	Range of shareholders predominantly Greek	Open	Small and medium sized companies, public and private	Up to £250,000	Yes	Exceptionally	No	Not under normal circumstances	Open	Flexible. Good performance would encourage continuing contact	Close working relationship with senior management to promote trust and without unnecessary involvement. No bank charges	Cannot be differentiated from total bank holdings
Commonwealth Development Finance Company Tel: (01) 407 9711	Several Commonwealth central banks and 160 major UK companies	£40 m or equivalent in foreign exchange	Investment in UK where there is strong overseas involvement, main involvement in overseas companies	£200,000 –£1 m equivalent	Yes with good short-term prospects	No	Yes, 10–49%	Not usually in UK, occasionally in overseas companies	Up to 10 years	Through local flotation or sale to partners. Looks for dividends. Discussed fully at outset	Highly flexible. All overseas expansions, mergers and takeovers considered	104 worldwide investments – £26.8 m
Co-operative Bank Tel: Manchester (061) 833 0299	Co-operative movement	Open	Corporate enterprises with emphasis on co-operative structures	Up to 50% of companies total financing requirement	Up to 50% of members/proprietors "matching" capital (maximum £25,000)	Exceptionally	No	No	Package comprising overdraft facilities, instalment finance and/or medium term finance	Repayment of loan	Servicing through national network of branches and head office specialised support	Several thousand corporate enterprises borrowing about £40 m
Council for Small Industries In Rural Areas (CoSIRA) Tel: Salisbury (0722) 24411	HM Government	£20 m	Companies with no more than 20 skilled employees in countryside or in towns with less than 10,000 population	£250–£50,000	Loans are available for new starters	Working capital loans are available	No	No	Building loans – 20 yrs. Working capital/equipment loans – 5 yrs	Repayment of loan	Availability of long term building loans. Local representatives throughout the country. Technical and business advice available	2,500 "live" loans – £16 m committed

(cont.)

Vehicle for Capital	Backers	Capital earmarked	Type of client or situation	Min/Max funds injected	Start up capital	Rescue capital	Equity stake	Seat on Board	Term of funding	Exit criteria	Special features	Portfolio
County Bank Tel: (01) 638 6000	National Westminster Bank	Open	Any growing company with track record: finance for the company, to enable shareholders to realise part of their investment, or to assist management in buying an equity stake	£50,000+	Exceptionally	Exceptionally	Yes, usually 10–20%	When invited	Loans up to 15 years, equity open	Prefers running dividend, realisation indeterminate	Informal management involvement; further substantial funds available if company is successful; other types of risk finance can be provided	81 companies – £7.4 m (at cost)
Development Board of Rural Wales Tel: Newtown (0686) 26965	HM Government Welsh Development Agency	Open	Manufacturing and service industries in mid Wales	£2,000–£1 m	Yes	Only by supporting new management in takeover situation	Yes	Yes	5–15 years – equity open	Sale by agreement with other shareholders	Range of advisory services. Outside businessmen appointed directors	177 companies £14.6 m
Development Capital Tel: (01) 486 5021	Co-operative Insurance, Commercial Union, Electra Investment Trust, NCB Pension Fund	Open	Proven management with prospects of growth. Both unquoted and quoted situations	£100,000 – £¾ m	Yes, with proven experience	Yes	Yes, to 40%	Yes, in participating non-executive capacity	3–5 years, including permanent capital	When appropriate to company's development programme or when convenient	Director's all ex-industry	14 companies – £6 m
Development Capital (NCDC) Tel: (01) 486 5021	Institutional funds	Open	Good track record £100,000 pre-tax profits potential	Up to £1 m	No	No	Participation in profits, but not necessarily direct equity	Yes	Up to 12 years	Repayment	Own experienced directors on board	14 companies – £3 m

(cont.)

Capital	earmarked	client or situation	funds injected	capital	capital	stake	Board	funding	criteria	features	
Estate Duties Investment Trust (EDITH) *Tel: (01) 928 7822*	£25 m Issued share capital	Listed authorized Investment trust, (managed by ICFC)	£5,000 – £1 m	No	No	Yes-minority, enabling shareholders to realise Investment	No	Provision of cash or exchange of shares for personal shareholders or family trusts	No time limit on duration of investment	Roll-over relief on CGT	200 companies – £20 m (by cost)
Equity Capital for Industry *Tel: (01) 606 2513*	Initially £42 m	City Institutions	£250,000 – £4 m	No	No	Yes, usually 10–25%	Usually, but depends on circumstances	Medium or long-term investment in equity or equity type conversion package	Flexible	Long term relationship with undertaking not to deal in shares	8 companies – £11m
European Investment Bank *Tel: (01) 222 2933*	At least £20 m for 1980	European Community operated by DoI and Scottish, Welsh and Northern Ireland offices	£17,000 – £2.5 m Maximum contribution is 50% of fixed asset cost of project	Loans can be made for sound projects by new companies with adequate equity	No	No	No	7 years including 2 year capital repayment moratorium	Not applicable	Priority to small and medium sized companies. EIB disburses in foreign currency but UK Government covers exchange risk. Fixed interest rate in region of 10%	Over £40 m lent since 1978 to about 100 companies
Federation Pension Fund *Tel: (01) 439 8546*	Open	The National Federation of Self Employed and Small Business, City of Westminster Assurance, Matthew Boys Group	£10,000 – £25,000	No	No	No	No	Up to 20 years	Repayment of loan	Available to Federation members only. Linked with competitive retirement benefit scheme. Available through Federation member brokers nationwide	First applications to be processed by summer 1980

(cont.)

Vehicle for Capital	Backers	Capital earmarked	Type of client or situation	Min/Max funds injected	Start up capital	Rescue capital	Equity stake	Seat on Board	Term of funding	Exit criteria	Special features	Portfolio
Gresham Trust *Tel: (01) 606 6474*	Gresham Investment Trust	Open	Profitable private companies looking for expansion, realisation of shareholders' interests, help for management in buying equity	Up to £500,000 May indicate larger amounts	Exceptionally	Exceptionally	Usually	Yes	Loans: 5–10 years Equity: Open	Looking for dividends	Gresham director on board. Other merchant banking facilities available	60 companies – £5 m
Hambros Bank *Tel: (01) 588 2851*	Hambros and institutional clients	Open	Good management track record either in proposed investment or previous companies	£100,000 –£2.5 m	Exceptionally	No	Yes	Yes	5–7 years	Looking for dividends	Panel of outside businessmen to take directorships	Cannot be differentiated from total bank holdings
Highlands and Islands Development *Tel: Inverness (0463) 34171*	HM Government (Scottish Office)	£15 m per annum	Manufacturing, tourist, agriculture, fisheries and other industries in the Scottish Highlands and Islands	Up to £400,000	Yes	Yes	Up to 40%	Exceptionally	5–10 years. 20 years for building loans	Equity by sale	Supplementary advisory and support services	3,000 businesses assisted
Industrial and Commercial Finance Corporation (ICFC) *Tel: (01) 928 7822*	Finance for Industry (Bank of England and clearing banks)	Open	Small and medium sized companies public and private	£5,000–2 m	Yes	Exceptionally	Yes, minority	Not under normal circumstances. Nominee director only with mutual agreement	Fixed interest loans medium and long term	Redemption negotiated individually, no requirement to sell shares	18 branch offices, leasing and hire purchase corporate advisory services, sale and leaseback facilities management consultancy	2,750 companies – £260 m

(cont.)

Vehicle for Capital	Backers	Capital earmarked	Type of client or situation	Min/Max funds injected	Start up capital	Rescue capital	Equity stake	Seat on Board	Term of funding	Exit criteria	Special features	Portfolio
James Finlay Corp Tel: *Glasgow* (041) 204 1321	James Finlay & Co.	Open	Energy-related industrial and service companies with prospects of growth, especially export	£50,000 –£250,000	No	No	Usually 20–49%	Yes	Usually loan/equity package	Flexible. Aim to capitalise by flotation or sale	Management advisory services and operational office in Houston, Texas	4 companies – £1 m
Local Enterprise Development Unit Tel: *Belfast* (0232) 691031	Dept of Commerce (Northern Ireland)	£5 m	Mainly manufacturing companies employing up to 50 people in Northern Ireland	£1,500 +	Loans, guarantees and grants available	"Maintenance packages" are provided	Yes	Not usually	Grants/loans /guarantees average 5 years	Repayment of loan or grants as required under terms and conditions of offer	Financial package tailored to requirements. Business, technical, marketing accountancy and design advice	Variable
Melville Street Investments Tel: *Edinburgh* (031) 226 4071	British Linen Bank and other financial institutions	£5 m	Profitable companies with good financial discipline	£50,000 –£500,000 May syndicate larger investments	Yes	Exceptionally	Minority	If asked	Long term capital	Flexible. Building up investment portfolio and does not seek to realise investments	Other merchant banking facilities available through British Linen Bank	25 companies – £3 m
Meritor Investments Tel: (01) 638 8861	Midland Bank, Rolls Royce Pension Fund	£4 m	Development situations and shareholders' needs	£100,000 –£250,000	No	No	Yes	Yes	Open	Dividend flow: sale when convenient to majority shareholders	Adaptability	New company

(cont.)

Vehicle for Capital	Backers	Capital earmarked	Type of client or situation	Min/Max funds injected	Start up capital	Rescue capital	Equity stake	Seat on Board	Term of funding	Exit criteria	Special features	Portfolio
Midland Bank Industrial Equity Holdings Group *Tel: (01) 638 8861*	Midland Bank	Open	Development situations and shareholders' needs	£5,000 –£200,000	Yes	Only in takeover situations or restructuring for capital transfer tax. Would back a new management	Yes	Usual	Open	Dividend flow: sale when convenient to majority shareholders	Adaptability	33 companies – £7.5 m
Minster Trust *Tel: (01) 623 1050*	Minster Assets	Open	Profitable private companies looking for expansion, realisation of shareholders' interests, management takeovers	£50,000 –£250,000	Exceptionally, where entrepreneurs have previous experience	Exceptionally	Yes, minority	Not under normal circumstances	Open	Flexible	Complementary advisory and support services	Small
Moracrest Investments *Tel: (01) 638 8861*	Midland Bank, Prudential & British Gas Pension Fund	£15 m	Development situations and shareholders' needs	£200,000 +	No	No	Yes	Yes	Open	Dividend flow: sale when convenient to majority shareholders	Adaptability	7 companies – £3.7 m
National Enterprise Board (NEB) *Tel: (01) 730 9600*	Public corporation financed by Parliament dividends and National Loans	Open	Manufacturing concerns as per statutory guidelines	As appropriate	Exceptionally	Exceptionally with long-term prospects	Yes	Reserve right to appoint own non-executive director	Longer term equity/loan package with maximum private sector involvement	Flexible	Small companies, regions, advanced technology and catalytic investments	Shareholdings 69 companies £1.25 bn Loans 35 companies £241.4 m

(cont.)

Vehicle for Capital	Backers	Capital earmarked	Type of client or situation	Min/Max funds injected	Start up capital	Rescue capital	Equity stake	Seat on Board	Term of funding	Exit criteria	Special features	Portfolio
National Research Development Corporation (NRDC) *Tel: (01) 828 3400*	UK Government through Treasury loans	Up to £50 m and revenue from successful projects	Development of new technology	Open	Yes, but for technical development not commercial start up	No	Often and if necessary but always at company's request	Depending on size of equity holding	Variable, funds recouped through royalties	When convenient to company. In joint venture financing, as soon as funds (inc interest service charges etc) are repaid	Technical patent, information and marketing services. No obligation to repay in event of failure	250 current industrial projects £30 m other development work
Noble Grossart Investments *Tel: Edinburgh (031) 226 7011*	Noble Grossart and Scottish Institutional shareholders	£7½ m	Proven management in growth sectors	£50,000 –£1 m	Yes, especially if the management has good track record in previous business	No	Yes, usually 20–40%	Yes with active non-executive participation	Open	Flexible but no requirement to sell	Emphasis on close working relationship with senior management	14 companies – £6 m
Rainford Venture Capital *Tel: St Helens (0744) 28882*	Pilkington Brothers, Community of St Helens Trust and others	£2 m	Entrepreneurs, primarily start-ups in St Helens	£50,000+	Primarily	No	Yes but preferably not control	If appropriate	Primarily equity. Loans where appropriate to agreed term	Equity – according to circumstances Loan – repayment	Advice on premises, accounting, labour, training, marketing and local services through Community of St Helens Trust	New company

(cont.)

Vehicle for Capital	Backers	Capital earmarked	Type of client or situation	Min./Max funds injected	Start up capital	Rescue capital	Equity stake	Seat on Board	Term of funding	Exit criteria	Special features	Portfolio
Scottish Development Agency (SDA) Small Business Division Tel: Edinburgh (031) 343 1911	UK Government	Open	Scottish manufacturing and service companies normally less than 100 employees outside the crofting counties	Up to £50,000 Larger sums available through SDA investment division	Yes	Exceptionally	Where appropriate most funding is through secured loans	If equity is taken, right to appoint a director	2–20 years equity open	By agreement with other shareholders	Management and technical services. Special interest rates available in certain circumstances	316 companies – £2.3 m
Smithdown Investments Tel: (01) 629 9891	Private individuals	Open	Start-up situations and very small companies	£5,000 –£50,000	Yes	No	Yes	By agreement	Open	Open	Financial management advice and someone to "bounce ideas off"	5 companies – around £200,000
Technical Development Capital (TDC) Tel: (01) 928 7822	ICFC	Not limited	Technology-based companies	£5,000 –£0.5 m	Yes	Exceptionally	Yes, minority	When appropriate	Fixed interest loans medium and long term	Redemption negotiated individually, no requirement to sell shares	Management support available through TDC developments	84 companies – £6 m
Welsh Development Agency Tel: Treforest (044 385) 2666	UK Government	Open	Welsh manufacturing and service industries	£2,000– £1 m	Yes	Only by supporting new management in take-over situation	Yes	Yes	5–15 years – equity open	Sale by agreement with other shareholders	Range of advisory services. Outside businessmen appointed directors	177 companies – £14.5 m

Abstracted from *The Investor's Chronicle*.

Appendix I
Glossary of the Key Terms Used in the Text

In each case a brief definition is given together with, where appropriate, a paragraph reference for a fuller description.

ACCEPTANCE CREDIT	A short-term advance against the security of a specific invoice.	(7, Table 14.2)
ACID TEST RATIO	Current assets excluding stock divided by current liabilities.	(Table 2.4)
ACCRUALS	The opposite of prepayments, being the unpaid element of expenses which are paid periodically at the end of the period to which they relate. Electricity bills are an example.	
AUDITED ACCOUNTS	Accounts which are independently verified.	(paragraph 2.2)
BREAK-EVEN	To be trading at neither profit nor loss.	(paragraph 10.4)
CALL	Money is at call if repayment can be demanded with no specific notice.	(paragraph 2.3.5)

Managing Your Company's Finances

CASH FLOW	The way in which monetary receipts and outgoings pass through a business. Net receipts are a positive cash flow, net outgoings a negative cash flow.	(paragraphs 1,2, 4.2)
CONVERTIBLE LOAN	A loan which can, in certain circumstances, be converted in whole or part into equity.	(paragraph 14.6.1)
COST PLUS PRICING	Pricing by adding a profit margin to the cost of the product.	(paragraph 12.6)
CREDIT CONTROL	The control of all the consequences of allowing a time-gap between sale and payments (relating to both customers and suppliers).	(paragraph 5.2)
CREDITOR	One who is owed money by the business, i.e. who has given it credit.	
CREDITOR PERIOD	The period between receipt of goods and the payment for them.	(Table 2.4)
CURRENT ASSET	An asset which will, or should, convert into cash within twelve months.	(paragraph 2.3.4)
CURRENT COST ACCOUNTING	A basis of preparing accounts using the current cost (rather than historic or actual cost) of replacing assets.	(paragraph 2.7)
CURRENT RATIO	Current assets divided by current liabilities.	(Table 2.4)
DEBTOR	One who owes money to a business.	

Appendix I

DEBTOR PERIOD	The time difference between a sale and the receipt of cash.	(Table 2.4)
DEFERRED TAX	Taxation which is not payable at a specific time but could become payable in certain circumstances.	(paragraph 2.3.6)
DEPRECIATION	A method for charging a proportion of the cost of wasting assets (and correspondingly reducing the balance sheet value of the asset) against profit.	(paragraphs 2.3.1, 3.2)
DISCOUNT RATE	The equivalent interest rate used in a discounted cash flow computation.	(paragraph 8.6)
DISCOUNTED CASH FLOW	A method of comparing receipts (less payments) of cash when there are timing differences based on the fact that cash in hand now is worth more than cash received in the future.	(paragraph 8.6)
DISTRIBUTABLE PROFIT	Profit after all deductions including tax. It is, in theory, available for distribution to shareholders.	(paragraph 3.2)
DIVIDEND	A periodic profit distribution made to shareholders in proportion to the number of shares held.	
DIVIDEND COVER	A measure of the security of dividend payments, being after tax profit divided by total dividend payments.	(Table 2.4)

DOUBLE ENTRY	The conventional method of book-keeping whereby every item is entered as a debit in one account and a corresponding credit in another account.	(paragraph 2.2.4)
EARNINGS	After tax profits, i.e. earnings for the shareholders.	
EQUITY	Any shares which participate in the profits of the company. Normally ordinary shares.	
FACTORING	The advance of finance against the security of specific invoices which are often forwarded to the financier for collection.	(3, Table 14.2)
FIXED ASSETS	Assets which are the basic resources of the business, and not for resale in the normal course of business but are held to earn revenue.	(paragraph 2.3.1)
GEARING		
(a) Capital	Total borrowings compared with the net worth of the business	(Table 2.4)
(b) Income	Total interest charges expressed as a percentage of pre-tax and pre-interest profit. It is a measure of the risk of borrowing.	(Table 2.4)
GOING CONCERN	An accounting concept which assumes the business will continue to trade.	(paragraph 2.2.3)
GOODWILL	A balancing figure, being the difference between net tangible assets and shareholders' funds.	(paragraph 2.3.7)

Appendix I

GROSS MARGIN	Gross profit as a percentage of sales.	(Table 2.4)
GROSS PROFIT	Sales less direct or variable costs relating to the sales but before deducting general overheads	(paragraph 3.5)
HIRE PURCHASE	A financing method whereby assets are hired from the financier for a period prior to the exercise of an option to purchase the assets for a nominal sum.	(5, Table 14.2)
HISTORIC COST ACCOUNTING	The conventional basis of accounting used exclusively prior to recent inflation accounting techniques. All assets are taken at historic cost less depreciation with no allowance due to increased value or replacement cost being made.	(paragraph 2.2.5)
INDIRECT COSTS	Costs which do not vary proportionately to sales or production levels.	(paragraph 10.7)
INVOICE DISCOUNTING	A form of factoring whereby finance is advanced against invoices but the company retains the control of debt collection.	(4, Table 14.2)
LEASING	A method of paying for an asset by hiring it on a contracted basis from the financier. The title to the equipment does not pass to the lessee.	(6, Table 14.2)
LISTED COMPANY	One whose shares are 'quoted' on The Stock Exchange.	

LONG TERM	Any finance of greater than approximately seven years' duration.	
MANAGEMENT ACCOUNTS	Accounts prepared by a company's management for their own use.	(paragraph 2.2)
MARK-UP	The percentage by which bought-in goods are increased in price before sale.	(paragraph 12.6.1)
MEDIUM TERM	Finance where duration is approximately three to seven years.	
NET MARGIN	Net profit as a percentage of sales.	(Table 2.4)
NET PROFIT	Profit after all deductions except tax.	
NET PRESENT VALUE	Today's equivalent value of a stream of future income as derived from a discounted cash flow analysis.	(paragraph 8.7)
OVERHEADS	Expenses which a business incurs and which tend not to vary with sales level, e.g. rent, electricity.	
PAYBACK PERIOD	The length of time for an asset to pay for itself from extra sales revenue.	(paragraph 5.2)
PREFERENCE SHARE	A share which receives its dividend (and return of) capital) in priority to other shares i.e. ordinary shares.	(paragraph 14.6.2)
PREPAYMENTS	The unused element of expenses which are paid periodically in advance. An example is rent paid six monthly in advance; two months after the payment	

Appendix I

	four months of rent is still accrued, i.e. not yet chargeable to the profit and loss account.	
PRICE EARNINGS RATIO	The ratio of the value of a listed company (number of shares times their stock market value) to the after-tax profits.	(Table 2.4)
PRODUCTIVITY	The efficiency of use of the resources of a business, particularly labour.	(paragraph 3.3)
REALIZATION	A basic accounting concept whereby profit is not taken on goods until they are actually sold.	(paragraph 2.2.6)
REPLACEMENT COST	The cost of replacing an asset at current prices.	(paragraph 2.7)
RETURN ON CAPITAL	The after-tax profits of a business expressed as a percentage of the assets employed in the business.	(Table 2.4)
SHARE CAPITAL	The finance subscribed by shareholders in a business in return for shares in that business.	
SHAREHOLDERS' FUNDS	The net worth to the shareholders of the business after settling all liabilities.	(paragraph 2.3.7)
SHORT TERM	Finance of less than approximately three years' duration.	
STOCK TURN	The number of times that stock is sold and replaced by each year. It is a measure of efficiency.	(Table 2.4)
TERMS OF TRADE	The length of credit given by a business to its customers.	

Managing Your Company's Finances

VARIABLE COST	A cost which varies in proportion to the level of sales or production.
VARIANCE	The deviation of actual performance from some budgeted figure.
WORK IN PROGRESS	Goods which are partly manufactured, i.e. on the shop floor at the time of a stock count.

Appendix II
Industrial and Commercial Finance Corporation Limited

AII.1 Introduction

ICFC was formed to provide longer-term finance to small and medium-sized British companies and is now well established as the chief source of such finance. It is not Government controlled (contrary to popular misconception) nor does it use Government funds. Through its parent company, Finance for Industry Ltd., it is owned by the UK Clearing Banks, and the Bank of England also has a small shareholding.

ICFC offers a complete financial service to its customers. When asked it will also provide practical advice and guidance on financial matters or on management but, as a corner stone of its policy, it never seeks to interfere with a customer's business. In the years between its formation and 1981 ICFC has supplied nearly £700 million to a total of over 7,000 British companies engaged in nearly every branch of industry and commerce.

The Corporation's financial philosophy is to offer packages which are tailor-made to suit the precise needs of the customer and these packages range from the simplest of mortgages to the most complex mixtures of loan and share capital. Contact with the Corporation can be made through any of its eighteen area offices sited in major business centres throughout Britain.

AII.2 The Scale of ICFC's Financing

ICFC will provide amounts as small as £5,000 in the form of loans, shares, hire purchase or leasing. At the upper end of the scale it will

Managing Your Company's Finances

provide £2 million or more. Its total investment outstanding by 1981 was around £400 million in some 3,400 companies. It will be seen from Table AII.5 that although the average investment is around £940,000, 54% by number of current investments are below £50,000. Some of these investments are, of course, the reduced balance of a larger investment but at the time of writing around 56% of all new investments still fall into this category.

To illustrate the spread of the Corporation's portfolio Table AII.6 gives a breakdown by industrial sector. Any application from any industry is considered on its own merits and the particular features of the spread illustrated are a function of accident rather than policy. For example, the small investment in the category gas, electricity and water is a result of this industry being dominated by nationalized and other substantial companies.

As an indication of the current scale of the Corporation's activities it completed transactions with 1,014 companies (involving a total investment of £96 million) in the financial year ended 31st March 1981.

AII.3 ICFC Investment: Uses

In broad terms ICFC will provide medium and long-term finance for any commercial purpose which makes financial sense. The standard areas of need in which the Corporation operates are as follows:

1. Cash required for a company's expansion or protection. This includes financing factories, plant, working capital, funding of bank overdrafts and balance sheet restructuring.
2. Cash which the shareholders require either because they wish to retire or because they wish to diversify into other ventures. This need often arises from the Capital Transfer Tax planning requirement of families owning substantial private companies. (This is often done through ICFC's associate company, Estates Duties Investment Trust Limited, EDITH, which is a listed investment trust).
3. Cash which is required to help managers acquire their own companies. This need usually arises from the receivership of a parent company or the wish of a parent or majority shareholder to divest itself of the company.
4. Long term financing requirements of professional operations which may be obliged by law to remain as partnerships. During the period of extremely high inflation in the UK many professional firms such as accountants found themselves unable

Appendix II

to finance the rapid increase in debtors from the profits of the firm. Often these increases were such that the bank was unable to continue providing full support.
5   Finance to get businesses started.

AII.4   ICFC Investment: Forms of Finance

The main types of finance offered by ICFC fall into the following broad categories though many individual deals consist of a mixture of individual components:

1   Hire purchase.
2   Leasing.
3   Loan finance which is characterized by being long term, namely five to twenty years.
4   Minority equity stakes.
5   Preference shares, both redeemable and irredeemable.
6   Property development and sale and leaseback facilities.

AII.5   Features of ICFC Investments

The Corporation prides itself upon the flexibility of its investment policy and goes to considerable length to tailor packages to individual requirements. However, there are certain standard features which are worth listing:

1   A firm policy of non-interference. The requirement for a nominee non-executive director is rare and is only taken in approximately 4% of investments.
2   All loans are at a fixed rate of interest which provides certainty of cost to the borrower.
3   Personal guarantees are not required.
4   A willingness to take equity by a subscription or purchase but no insistence on this in every case. At the present time some 60% of investment is not equity linked.
5   When equity is taken this will always be only a minority stake which may even have no voting rights, reflecting the non-interference policy.
6   A willingness, and often enthusiasm, to make further investments.
7   A willingness to consider start-ups and other high risk situations. For example 417 start-ups were financed in the year 1980/81.
8   A willingness to be locked in minority shareholdings indefinitely, only seeing a realization when the majority shareholders freely decide to sell out.

Managing Your Company's Finances

9   A willingness to invest in high technology situations (usually done through Technical Development Capital Limited, a wholly owned subsidiary).

AII.6   Other Services

1   *ICFC Consultants Ltd* – this is a subsidiary company which specializes in management consultancy for the smaller company. It also offers comprehensive training assistance and arranges many courses of interest to the smaller business man.

2   *Technical Development Capital Ltd.* (TDC) – this subsidiary company's function is to help entrepreneurs create new, or expand existing, businesses based on worthwhile technological innovation. A new development, whether product, process or service, can be supported at any stage but the closer it is to commercial realization the greater the likelihood of favourable assessment. A recently formed subsidiary, TDC Developments Ltd., will also provide help with management where this is necessary.

3   *Estate Duties Investment Trust PLC* (EDITH) – this listed company is managed by ICFC which also has a 42% shareholding. Its sole function is to purchase minority stakes in unlisted companies enabling shareholders to raise sufficient cash to meet tax and other personal liabilities without having to sell control. It does not require board representation or have a time limit on the duration of its investments.

4   *ICFC Corporate Finance Ltd.* – a fellow-subsidiary of the Corporation which provides advice and documentation work for listed companies. It will also assist with introductions for potential buyers or sellers of companies.

5   *Subsidized Finance* – at the time of writing the Corporation has a facility from the European Coal and Steel Community for expansion projects by small and medium-sized industrial companies in Britain. To be eligible a project need not be directly connected with the coal or steel industries but must be located in an area where redundancy has occurred in these industries and jobs must be offered to redundant workers. Interest rates are particularly attractive. Similarly, a subsidized line of finance from the European Investment Bank is available in certain development areas.

6   *Pension Fund Management* – it is ICFC's experience that many companies require a more personal and intimate pension service

Appendix II

than institutions managing hundreds of millions of pounds of funds can, or wish to, provide. To meet this need it has an experienced team who concentrate on the management of a limited number of smaller pension funds.

AII.7 Examples of ICFC Finance

The examples that follow are all real and give an indication of the scope of ICFC's financing.

AII.7.1 Small Business Loan

Business: Printers and typesetters
Proposal: The Company wanted long-term money to finance its increasing turnover.
Scheme: The finance provided was a £10,000 loan secured by a debenture on the Company's assets. Repayment of principal and interest by equal quarterly instalments over ten years was agreed.

Table AII.1 Summary of Trading Results for the 5 years prior to ICFC financing

Turnover	£145,000	£195,000	£235,000	£261,000	£325,000
Net Profit	£2,600	£3,100	£1,300	£1,400	£4,000

Balance Sheet Before ICFC Finance

Fixed Assets		
Plant, Machinery & Motor Vehicles		23,000
Current Assets		
Stock & Work in Progress	2,400	
Debtors & Prepayments	32,500	
	34,900	
Less: Creditors	41,400	
	(6,500)	
Less: Bank Overdraft	4,700	
		(11,200)
Net Tangible Assets		£11,800
Representing		
Ordinary Shares		1,000
Reserves		10,800
		£11,800

177

Managing Your Company's Finances

AII.7.2 Loan and Share Subscription

Business: Design, manufacture and assembly of underwater equipment.

Proposal: The Company wanted additional working capital for increasingly large contracts.

Scheme:

£55,000	Share Subscription
£45,000	Secured Loan to be repaid by ten annual instalments of £4,500
£100,000	

The scheme, in addition to providing long term capital, was designed to reduce the holding company's equity percentage from a controlling stake to a minority one, thus giving the management greater control.

Table AII.2 Summary of Trading Results for the 5 years prior to financing

Turnover	£221,000	£306,000	£347,000	£605,000	£640,640
Net Profit	£2,000	£24,000	£21,000	£18,000	£23,000

Note: The net profit is significantly understated as a result of payments made to the holding company.

Balance Sheet before ICFC finance

Fixed Assets		
Plant & Machinery, Vehicles and Fixtures & Fittings		34,800
Current Assets		
Stock & Work in Progress	283,800	
Debtors & Prepayments	66,400	
Bank & Cash	14,200	
	364,400	
Less: Liabilities		
Creditors & Accruals	199,200	
Directors' Loans	21,300	
Holding Company Loan	71,000	
	291,500	
Net Current Assets		72,900
		£107,700
Representing		
Ordinary Shares of £1		50,000
Reserves		57,700
		£107,700

Appendix II

AII.7.3   Share Purchase

Business: Retailers of menswear

Proposal: The Company was wholly owned by members of a family and family trusts. The shareholders wanted to realize some of their capital in order to meet taxation and other personal liabilities.

Scheme: The Company made a bonus issue from reserves of 100,000 Cumulative Convertible Participating Preferred Ordinary Shares. ICFC and EDITH jointly purchased the new Shares at an agreed premium from the shareholders who wanted to sell.

Table AII.3   Summary of Trading Results for the 5 years prior to the share purchase

Sales (£)	1,540,000	2,048,000	2,202,000	3,008,000	3,906,000	4,500,000
Profit Before Tax (£)	30,700	140,800	220,700	223,700	427,800	500,000

Summary of Balance Sheet

Balance Sheet before the bonus issue

Fixed Assets			
Land & Buildings			402,500
Fixtures, Fittings & Vehicles			226,100
			628,600
Current Assets			
Stock		1,398,300	
Debtors & Prepayments		215,400	
		1,613,700	
Less: Liabilities			
Creditors & Accruals	671,700		
Corporation Tax	145,900		
		817,600	
		796,100	
Bank Overdraft (Secured)		30,900	
Net Current Assets			765,200
			1,393,800
Less: Bank Term Loans			260,000
Net Tangible Assets			1,133,800
Less: Deferred tax			284,800
			£849,000
Representing			
Share Capital			300,000
Ordinary Shares			549,000
Reserves			£849,000

AII.7.4 Start-up

Business: Distributors of micro-computers.

Proposal: The company wanted money to purchase two demonstration micro-computers and needed substantial working capital to cover their first year of operation. The managers were able to provide £38,500 but needed a further £26,500.

Scheme:

£10,000	Leasing facility for the two demonstration micro-computers.
£15,000	Secured loan repayable over six years starting two years hence.
£ 1,500	Share subscription.
£26,500	

The managers' contribution was invested by way of preference and ordinary shares. The company's plan is to market a range of hardware and accounting software to professional accounting firms. The hardware and software have been produced by a major UK company.

AII.7.5 Helping Managers to buy their Business

Business: Specialist engineers

Proposal: The company was wholly owned by a foreign parent into whose industrial strategy it no longer fitted. The directors, who had all served with the company a long time, wished to buy but could only raise around £43,000; the agreed price was around £170,000.

Scheme: The difficulty with such a proposal was that S54 of the Companies Act 1948 prohibits a company from giving security in any form for the purpose of raising money to buy its own shares. In addition, as can be seen, the assets were fully required to satisfy the bank that its £250,000 trading facility was secure. These points dictated the final scheme which was that the directors subscribed £43,000 to a new holding company for Ordinary Shares, ICFC subscribed £27,000 for Convertible Preferred Ordinary Shares and also £100,000 for Redeemable Preference Shares whose redemption did not begin until after the parent loan was repaid. This scheme satisfied all parties and left an acceptable consolidated balance sheet.

Appendix II

Table AII.4 Summary of Trading Results for the 5 years prior to finance

Sales (£)	740,000	868,000	1,113,000	1,230,000	1,587,000	2,000,000
Profit Before Tax (£)	31,000	50,000	40,000	62,000	78,000	145,000

Summary of Balance Sheet

Balance Sheet before ICFC Finance

Fixed Assets

Land & Buildings		16,000
Plant, Fixtures & Vehicles		50,600
		66,600

Current Assets

Stock	350,200	
Debtors	526,700	
	876,900	
Less: Creditors	284,000	
	592,900	
Less: Bank Overdraft	255,700	
Net Current Assets		337,200
Net Tangible Assets		403,800
Less: Deferred Taxation		151,100
Shareholders' Funds		£242,700

Table AII.5 Gross facilities and gross advances by amount

	Outstanding at 31st March 1981				Gross Advances 1980/81			
	No.	%	£'000	%	No.	%	£'000	%
Up to £10,000	444	13.1	2,265	0.6	117	11.5	660	0.7
£10,001 to £20,000	482	14.2	7,467	1.9	124	12.2	2,054	2.1
£20,001 to £50,000	902	26.5	31,439	7.9	324	32.0	11,861	12.4
£50,001 to £100,000	621	18.3	45,368	11.3	223	22.0	16,844	17.6
£100,001 to £150,000	312	9.2	39,275	9.8	91	9.0	11,724	12.3
£150,001 to £200,000	166	4.9	29,465	7.4	30	2.9	5,348	5.6
£200,001 to £250,000	115	3.4	26,293	6.6	29	2.8	6,669	7.0
£250,001 to £300,000	64	1.9	17,655	4.4	15	1.5	4,260	4.4
£300,001 to £350,000	43	1.3	14,035	3.5	11	1.1	3,722	3.9
£350,001 to £400,000	47	1.4	17,906	4.5	6	0.6	2,306	2.4
£400,001 to £450,000	32	0.9	13,773	3.4	9	0.9	3,946	4.1
£450,001 to £500,000	38	1.0	18,353	4.6	9	0.9	4,808	5.0
£500,001 and over	134	3.9	136,768	34.1	26	2.6	21,502	22.5
Sub Total	3,400	100.0	400,062	100.0	1,014	100.0	95,704	100.0
Leasing and Hire Purchase	486*	—	51,411*	—	555	—	24,459	—
Total	3,886	—	451,473	—	1,569	—	120,163	—

*Additional customers only

Table AII.6 Gross facilities and gross advances by industry, £'000

	Outstanding at 31st March		Gross Advances	
	1981	1980	1980/81	1979/80
Agriculture, Forestry and Fishing	3,128	2,866	393	1,034
Mining and Quarrying	2,271	2,153	412	783
Food, Drink and Tobacco	15,051	12,740	2,833	3,860
Coal, Petroleum and Chemicals	9,605	8,038	2,165	3,153
Metal Manufacture	9,811	7,350	2,528	2,349
Mechanical Engineering	34,809	27,846	9,055	7,083
Instrument Engineering	8,943	7,806	2,171	3,176
Electrical Engineering	21,917	17,032	5,024	6,344
Shipbuilding & Marine Engineering	1,707	1,532	370	302
Vehicles	3,749	4,297	699	1,711
Metal Goods	19,100	15,312	5,043	4,681
Textiles	10,163	10,148	1,417	1,870
Leather	524	468	84	25
Clothing and Footwear	9,490	9,538	1,390	2,511
Bricks, Pottery, Cement and Glass	7,003	5,947	1,709	2,780
Timber, Furniture, etc.	10,385	9,971	1,874	1,911
Paper, Printing and Publishing	26,371	20,444	7,416	9,020
Other Manufacturing	15,327	11,470	5,362	2,887
Construction	26,051	23,201	5,728	9,741
Gas, Electricity and Water	1,199	1,209	30	—
Transport and Communication	20,700	18,073	3,294	6,651
Distributive Trades	50,799	47,176	9,247	14,186
Insurances, Banking and Scientific Services	62,132	53,846	15,363	10,599
Hotel and Catering	21,801	15,413	7,828	5,447
Miscellaneous Services	8,026	4,198	4,269	2,422
Total	400,062	338,074	95,704	104,526

Bibliography

Title	Most Relevant to Chapters	Author(s)	Publisher	Comments
Practical Corporate Planning	1	JOHN ARGENTI	George Allen & Unwin	A practical discussion of corporate objectives and planning.
Finance for the Non-Accountant	2 3 4	L E ROCKLEY	Business Books	Fuller but still simple discussion of accounting, cash flow, inflation, project returns and risk.
Financial and Cost Accounting for Management	2 7 8 9 10 11	A H TAYLOR	Macdonald & Evans	Fuller discussion of accounting including costing and information systems.
Capital Budgeting and Company Finance	3 8	A J MERRETT and ALLEN SYKES	Longman Group	A theoretical discussion of investment appraisal methods and risk. Full coverage of d.c.f. techniques.

Title	Most Relevant to Chapters	Author(s)	Publisher	Comments
Interfirm Comparison	3	HERBERT INGHAM and L TAYLOR HARRISON	William Heinemann	Fuller discussion of comparing practical aspects of company performances.
Control of Working Capital	4 5 6 14 15	Edited by MARTIN GRASS	Gower Press	Detailed discussion of working capital and stock and debtor management. Also covers sources of finance and exporting.
Managing the Survival of Smaller Companies	5 6	A C HAZELAND and A S REID	Business Books	Practical advice on the prevention and cure of business failure.
Bigger Profits for the Smaller Firm	3 12	E G WOOD	Business Books	Covers the main areas of concern to control profits including marketing, costing and productivity.
Corporate Planning and Budgetary Control	7 8 9 10 11 12	J BATTY	Macdonald & Evans	Includes a detailed and practical discussion on management information systems.

Title	Most Relevant to Chapters	Author(s)	Publisher	Comments
Equity and Loan Financing for the Private Company	13 14 15	MICHAEL SPRINGMAN	Gower Press	Covers sources and types of finance. Gives details on the types of share capital and agreements which might result in institutional investment.
Money for Business	13 14 15	—	Bank of England	A useful and cheap guide to types and sources of finance.
Dictionary of Management	Appendix I	DEREK FRENCH and HEATHER SAWARD	Gower Press	A comprehensive terminology guide.

ICFC publishes a range of free booklets aimed at giving practical advice to management on specific topics. These can be obtained from any Area Office. The most relevant to this book are as follows:

Appraising Capital Investment Proposals, Budgetary Control, Control Without Accounts, Cost Systems, Borrowing Money for Capital Projects, Management Information Systems, A Monthly Statement for Management, Computers for the Smaller Firm, Controls for the Smaller Manufacturing Company, Profit from Increased Productivity of People, Profit and Cash Flow Forecasting.

Index

Absorption costing, 117
  see also Costing
Acceptance credits, 144
Accounting, 8–30
  current cost, 19–23
  examples for different
    businesses, 28–30
  inflation, 18–23
  rate of returns, 79–81
Accounts
  audited, 8
  management, 8
  trading and profit and loss, 11,
    16–18, 97
Acid test, 23, 45
Advisers, 128–31
  see also Auditors
Assets
  current, 13, 43
  fixed, 11, 77
  intangible, 14
  liquid, 43
  net tangible, 14
Audited accounts, 8
Auditors, 27

Bad debts, 60–3, 65
Balance sheet, 11–16, 48
  current cost, 22
  forecast, 107

Bank
  clearing, 152
  merchant, 153
  overdraft, 14, 142
Borrowing ratio
  see Gearing
Breakeven chart, 98–9
Budgetary control, 72–6
Budgets, 4
  capital expenditure, 77–88, 109
  cost, 96–105
  production, 75, 109
  profit and loss, 107–12
  revision of, 111–12
  sales, 75, 108–9

Call, 14
Capital
  budget, 109
  cost of, 79
  expenditure, 77–8
  expenditure budget, 77–88
  long term (loans), 143
  long term (shares), 146–7
  medium term, 140–4
  return on, 24, 34, 39
  security, 131–3, 145
  share, 16, 32
  short term, 140
  structure, 139–40

Index

Capital (*Cont.*)
  working, 43
Cash
  collection, 56
  control
    see Credit control
  management, 3, 40–52, 53
  surplus, 50
Cash flow, 2, 3, 18, 40–3
  discounted, 82
  forecast, 46–81
Conservatism, 10
Consistency, 10
Control
  see also Budgetary control, Credit control, Financial control
  financial, 4, 46, 59–60
  periods, 5
Corporate
  objectives, 2, 114–5
  planning
    see Plans, Long term
Cost, 10
  based pricing, 116–8, 122
  budgets, 96–105
    current, 19–23
    direct, 99–101
    fixed, 97–8
    historic, 15
    indirect, 101–2, 110
    labour, 100–1, 110
  of capital, 79
    production, 60
    replacement, 15, 22
    research, 77
    variable, 98
Costing
  absorption, 117
  marginal, 117, 123–4
Cover
  dividend, 25
Credit
  check, 56
  factoring, 142
  risk insurance, 56–7
  terms of, 66
Credit control
  cash business, 54–5
  contracting business, 55, 58
  of purchase, 65–71
  of sales, 53–64
  sales invoice business, 54, 56
Creditors, 14, 26, 65
  average period of, 24
Current assets, 13, 43
Current cost
  accounting, 19–23
  balance sheet, 22
  profit, 22
Current liabilities, 14
Current ratio, 25, 43

Debtors, 13
  aged list of, 57
  average period of, 24
Debts, bad, 60–3, 65
Deferred tax, 14
Depreciation, 11, 16, 19, 22, 32–3, 42, 77
Difficult payers, 60
Difficult times, surviving, 69–70
Direct costs, 99–101
Discount rate, 82
Discounted cash flow, 82
Discounting, invoice, 143
Discounts, 58–9, 69, 116–7
Dividend cover, 25
Double entry, 9, 11

ECGD, 57, 152
Entity, 9

Factoring, credit, 142
Finance
  external, 6
  internal, 127–8
  raising, 126–38
    see also Raising finance

Index

sources of, 150–64
types of, 139–49
Financial
　see also Cash management, Credit control
　control, 4, 46, 59–60
　management, 1, 2, 40
Fixed assets, 11, 73
Fixed costs, 97–8
Forecasts, 5, 74
　balance sheet, 107
　cash flow, 46–8
　production, 92–5
　profit, 45
　rolling, 46
　sales, 47, 89–92

Gearing, 16, 25
　income, 25, 103
Going concern, 9
Good will, 15
Government support, 148–9, 153
Gross margin, 18, 24
Gross profit, 16
Guarantees, personal, 133

Hire purchase, 13, 141, 143
Historic cost, 15

ICFC, 134, 173–83
Income
　gearing, 25, 103
　　see also Gearing
　security, 133
Indirect costs, 101–2, 110
Individuals as financiers, 151
Inflation accounting, 18–23
Information
　see also Budgets, Credit control, Forecasts
　management, 4
　systems, 4
Institutions, financial, 153–64
Insurance companies, 153
Intangible assets, 15

Internal rate of return, 84–5
Investment decisions, 2, 6, 79–85
Investments, 13
Invoice discounting, 143

Labour costs, 100–1, 110
Leasing, 141, 143
Liabilities
　current, 14
　other, 14
Liquid assets, 43
Listing, stock market, 147–8
Loans, 143
　see also Capital, Short term, Medium term, Long term
Long-term capital
　see also Capital
　loans, 143
　shares, 146–7
Long-term plans, 5, 76

Management
　accounts, 8
　cash, 3, 40–52, 53
　financial, 1, 2, 40
　information, 4
　　see also Budgets, Credit control, Forecasts
Margin
　gross, 18, 24
　net, 18, 24
Marginal costing, 117, 123–4
　see also Costs
Market based pricing, 118, 123
　see also Pricing
Markets, 89–91
Mark-up, 119
Materiality, 10
Medium term capital, 140–44
　see also Capital
Merchant banks, 153
Monetary measure, 9
Money market, 51

189

Index

Net margin, 18, 24
  average for different industries, 38
Net present value, 82−4
Net tangible assets, 14

Objectives, corporate, 2, 114−5
Overdraft, 142

Payback, 81
Plans
  corporate, 5, 76
  long-term, 5, 76
  short-term, 5
Price earnings ratio, 25
Pricing, 91−2, 114−25
  cost based, 116−8, 122
  market based, 118, 123
Production
  budgets, 75, 107
    see also Budgets
  costs, 101
  forecasting, 92−5
Productivity, 33−4
Profit, 31−3, 41
  and loss accounts, 11, 16−18, 97
  and loss budget, 107−12
    see also Budgets
  current cost, 22
  forecast, 45
    see also Forecasts
  gross, 16
  net, 16
  retained, 18
  trading, 16
Profitability, 3, 31−9, 41
Provisions, 32

Raising finance, 126−38
  see also Finance
  common weaknesses, 136
  in times of crisis, 136
  presenting your case, 134
  what the lender looks for, 134−5
Ratios, 23
  borrowing
    see Gearing
  current, 25, 43
  price earnings, 25
  stock turn, 24
Realization, 10
Replacement cost, 15, 22
  see also Costs
Research cost, 77
Reserves, 16
Retained profit
  see also Profit
Return
  accounting rate of, 79−81
  average rate of, 79−80
  average rate of in different industries, 37
  internal rate of, 84−5
  on capital, 24, 34, 39
  versus risk, 35
Risk, 35, 129
  credit, 56−7
Rolling forecast, 46

Sale and leaseback, 144
Sales
  budget, 75
    see also Budgets
  forecast, 47, 89−92
    see also Forecasts
Security
  capital, 131−3, 145
    see also Gearing
  income, 133
    see also Income gearing
Share
  capital, 16−32
    see also Capital
  convertible preferred ordinary, 147

Index

ordinary, 146−7
preference, 146
Shareholders, 23, 150−1
Shareholders' funds, 14
Short-term
  capital, 140
    see also Capital
  plans, 5
    see also Forecasts
Sources and applications of funds statements, 18, 48
Sources of finance, 150−64
Stock relief, 14
Stock turn, 24
Stock value, 13
Suppliers
  payment to, 68
  selection of, 65

Surviving difficult times, 69−70, 136

Tax, deferred, 14
Terms
  credit, 66
  of trade, 3
Trading profit, 16
  see also Profit
Types of finance, 139−49
  see also Finance

Unlisted securities market, 148

Value, stock, 13
Variable costs, 98
Variances, 73, 96−7, 100

Working capital, 43
Writ, 60